Meeting the Needs of Students of ALL Abilities

CORWIN
PRESS

The Corwin Press logo—a raven striding across an open book—represents the happy union of courage and learning. We are a professional-level publisher of books and journals for K–12 educators, and we are committed to creating and providing resources that embody these qualities. Corwin's motto is "Success for All Learners."

Meeting the Needs of Students of ALL Abilities

How Leaders Go Beyond Inclusion

Colleen A. Capper • Elise Frattura • Maureen W. Keyes

CORWIN PRESS, INC.
A Sage Publications Company
Thousand Oaks, California

For information:

Corwin Press, Inc.
A Sage Publications Company
2455 Teller Road
Thousand Oaks, California 91320
E-mail: order@corwinpress.com

Sage Publications Ltd.
6 Bonhill Street
London EC2A 4PU
United Kingdom

Sage Publications India Pvt. Ltd.
M-32 Market
Greater Kailash I
New Delhi 110 048 India

Printed in the United States of America

Library of Congress Cataloging-in-Publication Data

Capper, Colleen A., 1960-
    Meeting the needs of students of all abilities: How leaders go beyond inclusion / by Colleen A. Capper, Elise Frattura, Maureen W. Keyes
        p.   cm.
    Includes bibliographical references and index.
    ISBN 0-7619-7500-4 (cloth: alk. paper)
    ISBN 0-7619-7501-2 (pbk: alk. paper)
    1. Inclusive education—United States.   2. School districts—United States.
  3. School management and organization—United States.   I. Frattura, Elise
  II. Keyes, Maureen W. III. Title
    LC1201 .C36 2000
    371.9'046—dc21   99-050561

This book is printed on acid-free paper.

                02   03   04   05   06   07   7   6   5   4   3

Production Editor: Denise Santoyo
Editorial Assistant: Kylee Liegl
Typesetter/Designer: Lynn Miyata
Cover Designer: Michelle Lee

Contents

List of Handouts

Preface

Setting: Conversation on a beach in South Florida between Colleen (first author of this book) and a highly successful fiction author. The author is also the parent of an academically advanced sixth-grade female who has refused to attend school for the past 2 months and a high-school-age son whose grades are less than ideal.

Author: So what's your book about?

Colleen: Creating and sustaining schools that work for each student.

Author: But schools have never been able to do that.

Colleen: I know. But I think it's possible.

Author: What's your thesis?

Colleen: It's pretty simple [but not easy]. Teachers teach to a range of students.

Author: (Silence, then) But it cannot all be done in one classroom. How can teachers meet the needs of girls and boys in one room? They are so different.

Colleen stalled for time to think. She was reminded of a well-known researcher she invited to speak at a conference she chaired. Keynoting the conference, the researcher scoffed and derided the conference title, "One System for All."

Is it really possible for each student's needs to be met in one school? In one classroom? What is wrong with letting specialists plug the classroom learning holes outside the classroom? What is the problem with establishing separate programs and even separate schools for students who are not successful, who do not fit, where they can receive the help they need?

The purpose of this book is to address these questions by describing practical strategies that educators (we include parents, students, administrators, and policymakers in this term) can use to create and sustain schools that are successful for all students without adding on expensive, reactive, and ineffective separate programs, classrooms, and schools. We divide these strategies into four major sections of the book: (a) shift from providing separate programs for a few students to providing excellent educational services for all students, (b) channel the standards movement into proactive teaching and assessment to ensure student success, (c) use funding and the law to support excellent services for all, and (d) view the process as a journey, not as a destination.

We believe that this book can serve as a handbook for educational practice that truly makes a difference in student learning. As such, all educators will find the book quite useful, including parents, administrators, teachers, school board members, and policymakers. This book is not just theory, but is based on practice in schools. University faculty will also find the book a breath of practical fresh air grounded in the most recent educational research about what works in schools. University instructors can use the book as a primary text in courses related to school leadership, the principalship, the superintendency, school improvement and educational change, and courses dealing with diversity, multicultural education, and special services. The book will also be quite useful for teacher educators as it provides a realistic portrayal of how the school and district can support excellent teaching.

Throughout the book, we offer lists of steps and practical strategies, along with overheads, handouts, and forms that can easily be copied for use in staff development institute days, faculty meetings, parent organization meetings, or university classrooms for educators to put these ideas into practice in their own schools and districts. We also include at the end of each chapter a self-assessment that individuals can use as tools to begin asking questions about their current practices, assessing their strengths and areas of growth, and determining the next steps to take.

We saw a need for this book from our educational experiences and research and from our experience as parents of school-age children. Although we have participated in and witnessed countless examples of student success, we continue to see too many—far too many—students failing, often at the hands of educational reform.

For example, Colleen's son attended a school that was designed and functioned in a way that many educators would call "ideal": multiage classrooms not dependent on student grade level; thematic integrated instruction; peer mentoring and teaching; cooperative groups; students given time to learn what they need to learn, resulting in no pressure on students or competition between them; academic and social goals individualized for the student and cowritten with the teacher, student, and parent; a classroom and school culture that emphasize belonging and community; and performance-based assessment instead of standardized tests. So what was the problem? All students in this setting were not successful. Parents of graduates of this school recalled how ill-prepared their children were for high school, especially in mathematics and study skills. Other parents were concerned that their children's reading and writing skills were far below those appropriate for their children's age/grade level.

Colleen believed that her son needed something different, and before he experienced frustration or failure, he transferred schools. He needed structure to his day and separation between tasks and subjects. He needed someone to teach him directly the skills and knowledge he needed to know in addition to observing, interacting, and following his own learning instinct. His parents needed to know he was progressing where he needed to be at grade level. They knew the research was clear: Early intervention for academic skills is essential. If they had waited, he would have lost valuable time—measured in years.

The school he transferred to also had several characteristics of what many educators would consider the "ideal": a small school of one grade per class; small class size, with 14 students in his class; an emphasis on belonging and community; clear expectations for student achievement; a structured, sequential curriculum that was culturally integrated; high expectations for parent involvement that were met; and nightly homework. Colleen volunteered in her son's second-grade classroom half a day per week. By the end of the school year, however, not all of the students in this classroom were successful either. Although her son was thriving, 2 students in his class of 14 became disengaged to the point at times of not wanting to come to school. Several students struggled with basic skills in reading and math.

These examples show that neither school—one taking a holistic, progressive education approach, the other a "back to basics," high-expectations approach—reached each of its students. Educators have assumed for years that students learn best when the information is presented to them in specific ways (e.g., holistically, a "core curriculum"). In these schools, as in most schools, if students struggle with their learning, then to receive help they must be segregated from their peers and receive services from specialized staff, trained differently and from different university programs, to work with different children. This book argues against this assumption. Further, parents should not have to transfer their children to different schools, hire private tutors, or seek segregated programs to meet the needs of their children.

Despite the students' struggles in these two different schools, we disagree with the author on the beach: Each student's needs can be met, in what we term *integrated educational environments*. As we explain in more detail later in the book, we do not oppose students receiving small-group or individual instruction outside the classroom. We do, however, advocate that each day *each* student should have the opportunity to receive small-group or individual instruction, whether this takes place in the classroom, the hallway, the bandroom, the school forest, a vocational work site, or the neighborhood library. Typically, however, the same individual or group of students leaves the classroom or the school to attend special programs while the rest of the students do not. This book describes not only why this is a problem but also why such integrated educational environments to meet the needs of students of all abilities are crucial and how to create and sustain these settings.

Description of Contents

We agree that educators can meet students' individual learning needs. Educators must meet them, however, in a way that honors and respects students and does not violate the norms of belonging. We can meet the needs of children without isolating them from their peers. In Chapters 1, 2, and 3, we discuss why this is important and how to begin making this happen. We propose proactive, preventive strategies for action, setting the stage for students to succeed before they fail—and for not requiring students to fail before they receive appropriate educational services.

Shifting from providing programs for a few students to providing services for all students to meet their individual needs requires a shift in educator roles (Chapter 4). The National Research Council (NRC; 1998) argues that "there is little evidence that children experiencing difficulties learning to read, even those with identifiable learning disabilities, need radically different sorts of supports than children at low risk, although they may need much more intensive support" (p. 3). This report and other recent research argue against the assumption that students who struggle in school require *specialists* in separate programs to teach them. Each student does, however, require excellent teaching in order to succeed. Indeed, the NRC reports, "Excellent instruction is the best intervention for children who demonstrate problems learning to read" (p. 3). Other research agrees. Citing a large-scale study of student achievement in Texas, Darling-Hammond and Falk (1997) report that "the single most important measurable cause of increased student learning was teacher expertise, including teachers' preparation and experience levels" (p. 193).

Educators cannot achieve excellent teaching alone, however; they need ongoing support for their efforts. In Chapter 5 we discuss how school principals can ensure student success and include the forms of support and the kinds of assurance that teachers need to be successful. Like students, we cannot expect teachers to practice excellent teaching without providing them the school and district conditions to ensure success. Further, unlike other books, our book shows how some administrative structures of schools might change to prevent academic failure. Specifically, the central office administration must model the changes it seeks in the schools, and in Chapter 6 we delineate strategies for doing so.

Although we are not totally enthusiastic about the standards-based reform that is sweeping the country, with our own children's education we have directly experienced how a lack of standards, obscure expectations, and inadequate assessment can thwart academic success and rob a child's self-esteem. In Part II of the book, we show how standards can pave the way for the success of all students. The first priority for standards, however, must be physical and emotional safety (Chapter 7). In Chapter 8 we outline six stages that educators need to consider when establishing curriculum standards. Because research is clear that teaching quality is the primary predicator of student success, in Chapter 9 we describe standards-based teaching that takes into account student learning diversity. We agree that student assessment is crucial for student success, and in Chapter 10 we present a multidisciplinary perspective of standards-based assessment. Although academic standards are crucial for all students, we also need to hold high expectations for student behavior. In Chapter 11 we identify specific standards that educators must hold for themselves and their students that pave the way for many proactive strategies beyond expulsion and suspension.

Often, educators view the law and funding as two primary barriers to educational change. In Part III, we provide examples of how important it is to understand how to move beyond legally mandated separate programs (Chapter 12). We also offer suggestions in Chapter 13 on ways that funding can remove barriers to services for students.

Given our two beliefs about change, we find it ironic (perhaps some would say hypocritical) to have written a "how-to" book. First, we believe that we cannot change anyone. We can only change ourselves (see Part IV, Chapter 14). Like a gardener who cannot force a seed to sprout, what we can do is create the conditions for change. We can plant, water, weed. We can encourage, nurture, support. This book is about creating and sustaining the conditions for change. We also believe that anyone can tend the garden of the school. Thus anyone can take the lead: parents, policymakers, students, principals, superintendents, teachers, and assistant principals, among others.

Second, we also believe that change is never ending. We take seriously that the root word of *education* is *educari*, which means to bring into healing (Remen, 1996). Thus we are constantly in a process of change and, if guided by a greater good, a constant process of healing. Although we consider this book a how-to, we do not consider it a "recipe" for change—that if you follow the directions exactly, you can change your educational situation. What we simply offer is our collective experience, strength, and hope of more than 57 years in education in our roles as general and special education teachers, reading teachers, teachers of students considered "at risk," principals, directors of special education, university professors and researchers, teachers of students considered gifted, students ourselves of ongoing learning, and most important as parents of children, all of whom have not "fit" the typical school system in one way or another.

Why "Beyond Inclusion"?

We also bring to this book our collective experience in working with students who have struggled in some way, including students with labeled disabilities within a variety of settings: residential institutions, segregated schools, segregated classrooms within schools, alternative schools, schools-within-schools, resource rooms, segregated camp settings, consultation models, and schools and districts that strove to include all students fully.

The inclusion movement in the past decade has asked the classroom teacher to be successful with all students in his or her room, including students labeled with a disability. Opponents argue, however, that it is better to let teachers do well what they do well. If a child is not successful, send the child out of the classroom to a teacher who can meet that child's needs. Likewise, inclusion proponents have expected all schools to meet all their students' needs in their attendance areas. Others assert, however, that maybe we should let particular schools do well what schools do well (e.g., college prep, arts magnet schools), and for those students who are not successful, allow them to attend other schools (e.g., in other districts, magnet schools, charter schools, alternative schools). As one principal of an alternative high school told us, "Students and parents need options, and the typical school cannot provide all the options."

This book addresses the concerns of those who do not favor inclusion. We have been disappointed, however, in the inclusion literature and practice. Although the inclusion literature sometimes mentions student needs other than disabilities, the main focus is students with disabilities. Even though this literature has made significant contributions to the field, it can perpetuate the very phenomena the authors wish to dissolve—that is, separating students, current practices, and school change into "general education" and "special education," and what each must do differently can serve to reinforce and maintain the separate practices (see Neville, 1999). Moreover, inclusion advocates sometimes dissolve into debates among themselves about whether each student should be "fully" included or included just part of the time. To lead beyond inclusion, we must move beyond these debates to learn how curriculum and instruction, leadership practices, and school structure might need to change to meet the needs of students of all abilities.

Here, we focus our efforts on the range of students who struggle in school because of racism, poverty, gender, sexual orientation, high aptitude, inattentive parents, low self-esteem, or other issues. Ultimately, we agree with the NRC (1998) that *"prevention* efforts must reach *all* children" (p. 16, italics added). The NRC argues,

> To wait to initiate treatment until the child has been diagnosed with a specific disability is too late. . . . Academic success, as defined by high school graduation, can be predicted with reasonable accuracy by knowing someone's reading skill at the end of grade 3. . . . A person who is not at least a modestly skilled reader by the end of third grade is quite unlikely to graduate from high school. (pp. 16, 21)

We must not wait until students experience failure before meeting their needs. Our research and experiences tell us that we cannot afford to wait. This book explains what to do instead of wait, and how to take action.

An Invitation: Not the Definitive Answer, Always More Questions

Much appreciation goes to the students in our university classes and for our conversations with educators in the field for all their creative ideas, for challenging us, and for being honest with their struggles and triumphs in their day-to-day work in schools. Not all the ideas in this book are new, but we hope that putting the ideas together in one place will be helpful. The perspectives we share here present our current thinking and practice in the sweltering Midwest heat of the summer of 1999. We do not pretend to have all the answers. Our promise is to continue asking ourselves and others questions, and from those questions new ideas or a reframing of previous ideas in this book will emerge. We welcome you to join us in the conversation by contacting us and sharing your experiences with meeting the needs of students of all abilities in integrated educational environments.

Acknowledgments

We appreciate the enthusiastic response and unfailing support of Robb Clouse, Acquisitions Editor, and Gracia Alkema, President of Corwin Press, for helping us bring this book to fruition. The Corwin staff were always helpful and efficient; many thanks to Denise Santoyo, production editor, and Linda Poderski, copy editor. We are grateful to the staff, students, and parents in the Verona Area School

District, Verona, Wisconsin, for taking steps to lead beyond inclusion. This book also could not have been completed without the institutional support of the University of Wisconsin–Madison in the form of a sabbatical leave for Colleen. We also appreciate the assistance of Madeline Hafner and George Theoharis, doctoral students in the School of Education at the University of Wisconsin–Madison, for tracking down data, references, and resources. Madeline also lent her eye for detail to a thorough editing of the galleys. Thank you! Colleen worked on much of this book while being with her seriously ill father 500 miles from Madison. She thanks the Department of Educational Administration at Madison and Allen Phelps, Department Chair, for providing laptop technology and e-mail and for expressing care and concern, all of which made this book possible. Pat Nehm, Department Program Assistant, came through with flying colors, as always, in the final days of manuscript preparation, transcending the physical miles between us. Colleen also thanks her son, Quinn, and her partner, literary novelist Bridget Birdsall, for giving up time with her in the final weeks of manuscript preparation, for their patience, and for bearing the sometimes intense moments that come from trying to meet deadlines. The contributions of the following reviewers are also gratefully acknowledged:

Pamela Beach
St. Elizabeth Ann Seton Elementary School, Oshkosh, WI

Leonard C. Burrello
Indiana University, Bloomington, IN

Kathy Entrekin
Exeter Township School District, Reading, PA

Gloria Ladson-Billings
*Professor, Curriculum Development and Instruction,
University of Wisconsin–Madison*

Debra Jackso
Superintendent, New Salem Schools, New Salem, NY

Linda Skrla
Texas A&M University, College Station, TX

Susan Smethurst
Carleton Village P.S. North, Toronto, Ontario

Carol L. Spencer
Best Practice Designs, Addison, VT

Virginia Stead
Lakehead University, Thunder Bay, Ontario

John T. Thompson
West Valley Central School, West Valley, NY

About the Authors

$\mathscr{C}$olleen A. Capper is Associate Professor in the Department of Educational Administration at the University of Wisconsin—Madison. She has published nearly 100 papers in the form of refereed journal articles, book chapters, and refereed and invited conference papers. Her previous book, *Educational Administration in a Pluralistic Society* (1993), is widely used in educational administration courses. A former special education teacher and administrator in Appalachia, her line of inquiry over the past decade has focused on the intersection of school leadership and issues of equity and diversity. Her most recent work examines the role that spirituality plays in the lives of leaders who lead for justice. She teaches the courses Leadership and Inclusive Schooling, Student Services and Diversity, Organizational Theory, and Spirituality in Leadership. She works with school districts across the country to better meet the needs of all students.

$\mathscr{E}$lise Frattura received her PhD from the University of Wisconsin—Madison, where her research focused on teachers as leaders. For more than 10 years, she has served as Director of Student Services, advocating for students who struggle in schools. She also is Lecturer at the University of Wisconsin—Madison and Milwaukee in leadership and inclusive schooling courses. A prolific grant writer, she has garnered more than $1 million in grants for her school districts. She has cowritten several refereed journal articles with Lou Brown, and has presented her work at several hundred conferences for practitioners. She consults regularly with school districts to help them move from programs to services to meet the needs of each student.

$\mathscr{M}$aureen W. Keyes, a former Special Education teacher and high school principal with 20 years' experience in the public schools, currently serves as Assistant Professor in the Department of Exceptional Education at the University of Wisconsin–Milwaukee. To this book, she brings her in-depth experience from working in the Milwaukee Public Schools, formerly as a teacher and now as a faculty-school liaison in the Urban Collaborative Partnership program. Her research and writing focus on the ways school leaders can create and sustain inclusive schools and, in turn, support students with challenging behaviors in schools. She is working on a book with Colleen Capper that reports on their exploration of the role spirituality plays in the lives of leaders leading for justice. She has published book chapters and articles in many refereed journals, including *Educational Administration Quarterly*, *Teacher Education*, and *Journal for a Just and Caring Education*.

To our children
for their wisdom, humor, patience,
and their innate sense of love for living:
Quinn
Sydney and Addyson
Matthew and Eric

Introduction

In this book, we address our ideas and strategies to *all* students. We define *all* students in a broad and inclusive way. To meet the needs of all students, educators must make it obvious that they include everyone and therefore that they value everyone's diversity, including students from traditionally privileged categories (e.g., white, male, middle class). The way educators define *all* and *diversity* must make it obvious to all who come in contact with the school that everyone in the school values and respects each person's diversity (Lodon, 1996).

Further, we believe that all people (students and staff) have a continuum of needs—physical, social, intellectual, emotional, and spiritual—that fluctuate and vary over time, depending on circumstances and situations. These needs are never stable but, rather, are constantly evolving and changing. As such, we often do not agree with the language of opposites usually associated with the terminology in education, such as typical/atypical, disability/nondisability, at-risk/not at risk, gifted/not gifted, students of color/white students. For example, we believe that all individuals—children and adults—are "at risk" at some point in their lives. We believe that all people have unique gifts and talents. We believe that all individuals are challenged in various ways that could disable them in some situations (e.g., managing money, social skills, intimate relationships, parenting). As such, we write this text to move beyond categories, not to homogenize individuals but to assert that "we are alike" while "we are each unique."

By focusing on education, we are well aware that this book examines only one piece of the interlocking system that includes the lives of our students. We do not address in-depth the crucial role that families, the community, religious institutions, universities, the media, and the medical field play in the lives of students. With our locus of control in education and to maximize our efforts, we can only act on what is in front of us and be clear about what we have the power to change and what we are powerless over.

What, if any, fundamentals does each student need to reach his or her maximum learning potential despite his or her learning style, race/ethnicity, gender, sexual orientation, social class, intelligence, or other characteristics? We have found that the following activity serves as a useful tool to begin addressing this question and to begin meeting the needs of students of all abilities.

Activity 1: "Each Student Learns Best When . . ."

As an individual or with a group of people, brainstorm a response to the following open-ended sentence:

We know that each student learns best when . . .

Expect the brainstorm to take up to 1 hour; it is best not to go longer than that. Record everyone's responses on newsprint or in a format that allows all to view the results. At the next meeting, build consensus on the list; either have the entire group work on the list or have small groups work on sections of the list. To do so, use the "fist to five" method of consensus building. Ask whether everyone agrees with each descriptor. Point to the first descriptor and ask to what extent each person agrees with that descriptor. It is important not to have discussion on each item. A fist means "I cannot agree," all five fingers up means "I am in full agreement," with fewer fingers meaning lesser degrees of agreement. Mark the descriptors for which all participants hold up three, four, or five fingers. Set aside the descriptors on which there is disagreement. Descriptors on which there is agreement/mixed agreement can serve as discussion items at later meetings. Descriptors on which there is widespread disagreement may be set aside for now.

Next, categorizing the agreed-on descriptors under major headings is often helpful, such as curriculum, instruction, social/emotional, and services, among others. Finally, we can compare our list with similar lists supported by research, such as the list of external and internal assets developed by the Search Institute (see Resource A). Of course, this activity may be adapted for your specific needs, such as group size and time.

The list that you or your group generates and agrees on should be typed up and copied for all participants. Gaining clarity about how each student learns best is a crucial first step. The rest of this book will help you translate into action this internal wisdom about what works for students.

Part I

Shift From Programs to Services

In Part I, we explain why and how to evolve from providing programs to providing services. In Chapter 1, we briefly describe the social and legal impetus behind such action. In the next two chapters, we then suggest two stages for moving from programs to services. In Chapter 2, we address the first stage: asking necessary questions. In Chapter 3, we address the second stage: developing teams to respond to the questions. In Chapter 4, we describe how, when shifting from programs to services, educator roles must evolve to meet the needs of students. Educators need support for these changes, and in Chapters 5 and 6 we discuss the significant role the school principal and the central office must play in this educational shift.

Chapter 1

Setting the Stage

The Social and Legal Impetus for Services Rather Than Programs

During the past 20 years, school districts across the country have homogeneously grouped into separate programs those children who they perceived needed additional assistance. When organizing these programs, district administrators considered funding sources, legal parameters, and space. Educators developed programs for students with disabilities by categories (e.g., learning disabilities, cognitive disabilities, emotional disabilities). In addition, legislation began to emerge that was sometimes paired with funding sources for other "troubled" populations, resulting in segregated programs such as alcohol and other drug abuse (AODA), Title I, English as a second language (ESL), students considered "at risk," teenage parents, students considered gifted, and homeless children. Specialized programs became a convenient way for adults to provide services.

Districts continue to administer each special program (e.g., ESL, at-risk, special education, or even programs inside a program—for example, emotional disabilities) in isolation from each other—as if each program is an island by itself. Administrators, department heads, and coordinators are assigned the oversight of specific programs, and most often such program monitoring is completed in isolation from others. Therefore each program evolves as an individual island of support; that is, each program has its own referral system, evaluation system, eligibility criteria, service parameters, and exit criteria. Often, programs set up parameters of "no service overlap"; that is, if students qualify for one, they may not receive services from any other. Special education and Title I services are examples of such programs. Parents, students, and even staff are forced to unravel the qualifiers around each program and to determine potential student referrals and eligibility.

Students challenge the programs and break the molds, general educators ask for increased support for behaviorally challenging students, and students are unable to meet the rigorous academic standards unfolding in every classroom. Support personnel are frantically attempting to bandage systemic wounds with the only isolated service bandages they control on their island. It is not working. As shown in Handout 1.1, educators continue to set up a model of short-term fixes for systemic problems, which results in exactly that—short-term fixes—while the underlying wounds continue to ooze. Educators certified in "special areas" (e.g., at-risk, special education, guidance, social work) are required to intervene after a student has experienced failure to resolve the issue or to put a modified bandage in place.

Typically, we meet the needs of students by building programs one by one instead of by moving together to develop a framework of services for all students (see Handout 1.2). Student needs increase, and we add more separate slots and programs (see Handout 1.3). We must move beyond the cosmetic change of programs to authentic change (Quinn, 1996). We need to admit that the short-term fixes do not work, never have and never will, and to take action toward remedying the underlying disease: education that does not work.

We identify six assumptions that many educators hold about separate programs (see Handout 1.4):

Assumption 1: We can better serve students who struggle if they are separated from their peers.

Assumption 2: We can only provide individual attention and support in a setting or situation separate from the student's peers.

Assumption 3: Staff are incapable of teaching to a range of students.

Assumption 4: Schools are incapable of changing to meet student needs.

Assumption 5: The locus of student problems lies within the student; thus, we have no need to examine a student's history to determine how we might deliver services to avoid student struggles.

Assumption 6: Students are more different than alike.

The research and our experience suggest at least eight major problems associated with these assumptions and with providing "programs" for students—programs that are characteristically identified by requiring students to be isolated within their classroom, removed from their classroom, or removed from their school (see Handout 1.5). These programs can include schools-within-schools, alternative schools, and charter schools established for students considered at risk. These problems can be correlated with assumptions about the ways educators currently function when meeting student needs.

First, separate programs perpetuate tracking of students of color and students of lower social class. Usually, the demographics of students enrolled in alternative programs, special education, and at-risk programs are overrepresented by students of color and of lower social classes. Research on effective teaching shows that students in these programs often do not have access to high-quality teaching and learning (Darling-Hammond & Falk, 1997; see also Chapter 9, this volume). Separate programs often limit these students' opportunities for further education beyond high school.

Special education, special programs (e.g., ESL, gifted education), and other alternative programs have become separate systems with separate funding, separate staff and materials, and a learning environment separate from other students. We advocate for "one system for all" because we believe that all students of all abilities (regardless of social class or color) can be successful within one school system. We agree that "one size" of instruction does not fit all students. If we offer a differentiated curriculum, instruction, and a variety of assessments and other creative strategies, however, as explained throughout this book, we can meet the needs of students of all abilities. Too often, we use the phrase "one system cannot do it all" as a reason to segregate students (often by social class or race) into separate programs. We can meet students' needs without establishing entirely separate systems.

Second, providing separate programs is quite costly fiscally, often pitting program advocates against each other over scarce resources. For example, special programs cost 130% more than general education; for example, if a school district spends $5,000 per student, then each student labeled for special programs costs the district $11,500 (Odden & Picus, 2000). A separate program means that students often require separate space, separate materials and infrastructure, a separate teacher, and an administrator not only to manage the program but also to spend time and money on organizing the program.

Third and relatedly, educators then spend an inordinate amount of time and resources deciding exactly for which program a student may qualify. In the Verona (Wisconsin) School District in 1999, for example, it cost more than $2,000 to evaluate one student to determine eligibility for special education. A district of 4,500 students averages 225 (5%) evaluations per year for a total of $443,713 spent on evaluations (see Handout 1.6). Other data confirm the cost differences between serving students within general education and serving them within separate programs. Chambers, Parrish, Lieberman, and Wolman (1998) report that total instructional expenditures for students at the elementary/middle school level who are served in the general education classroom are $3,920. If we serve these same students 25% to 60% outside the regular class, then the cost increases to $5,122. If we provide a program for these students in a separate public facility, like many charter and alternative schools, then the cost increases to $6,399 per student. We do not make this point about cost to imply that the major reason to move from programs to services is cost savings. For example, if we meet students' diverse learning needs by providing services, then we will need all the staff who previously served separate programs to make this a reality (see Chapter 9). Reallocating staff and resources into excellent instruction for all students in integrated environments will bring about a much greater return on our education investment.

Fourth, separate programs result in some students receiving services and other students not. One parent shared with us her frustration of the school slotting her child for special programs yet ignoring his needs at the same time:

> I have an 8-year-old now in second grade . . . who is still struggling as a reader. I was totally frustrated with the school's approach— essentially, that he needed more time—and our family was not needy enough for him to merit specialized services such as Reading Recovery. Throughout first grade (which was totally miserable for him), he was read to by volunteers, and he was part of Title I and hated it because of the self-esteem issue and essentially made no progress. Even though the Title I teacher has a master's degree in reading, he was just receiving "more of the same type of instruction" as in the classroom, when what he needed was another multisensory approach heavy in phonetics. We even paid to have an evaluation done that showed a mild learning disability, but the school ignored this. We were forced to use an outside reading tutor who in 3 months brought our child up to grade level and will probably have to do this again at the end of second grade since he is not receiving specialized reading instruction in school. I really feel for those families without the resources to do this.

As we can see from this example, students labeled with disabilities receive services, and students labeled as gifted receive services. Students who do not receive a formal label, however, do not receive services, or else we slot the students into "options" (e.g., volunteer tutors, Title I) that do not meet the students' individual learning needs.

Fifth, separate programs fragment a student's day. The students who often need the most structure, routine, consistency, and predictability in their day are often the students who must leave in the middle of a class to attend a special program.

Sixth, establishing separate programs not only drains the energy of staff but, in so doing, also conveys to an entire generation of students over and over again that they do not fit our system, not that the system has missed the mark with them. The National Research Council (NRC, 1998) agrees:

> Evidence from case study evaluations of children referred for special education indicate that instructional histories of the children are not seriously considered. . . . Rather, when teachers refer students for special services, the "search for pathology" begins and assessment focused on the child continues until some explanatory factor is unearthed that could account for the observed difficulty. (p. 27)

We as educators tend to focus on what is wrong with students rather than on what the school can do differently. Then, we assume that we must diagnose students and separate them from their peers or pull them out of class for special instruction. We do this even when, by doing so, we teach students that they are different, that they do not fit in, and that they will never be successful, compared with those students whom we have not categorized.

Seventh, special programs often serve an enabling function; that is, educators look to these special programs for solutions to "fix" students rather than examine more deeply how they can prevent student learning problems. As long as special programs exist, educators need not look at their own roles, policies, and practices in educating students and therefore need not make any changes. University training programs often reinforce this enabling function by emphasizing the "coordination of special programs" or understanding the intricacies of programs (e.g., AODA) or roles (e.g., guidance counselors) without offering tools or viewpoints to question and look beneath these programs and roles. As a result, administrators can end up working very hard making special programs more efficient or more coordinated without questioning the need for the programs in the first place. Tomlinson (1999) agrees and explains:

> Schools have tried to meet the needs of struggling and advanced learners by pulling them from regular classrooms for part or all of the school day. They were assigned to special classrooms with similar students and teachers who have the knowledge and skill to meet their unique needs. In full accord with common sense and classroom experience, much of the best research suggests that for struggling learners, such homogeneous learning experiences go awry. . . . Too often in these settings, teachers' expectations for the struggling learners decline, materials are simplified, the level of discourse is less than sterling, and the pace slackens. Too few students escape these arrangements to join more "typical" or advanced classes. In other words, remedial classes keep remedial learners remedial. (p. 21)

An eighth and related problem with special programs is the lack of transfer of educator and student knowledge and skills from the separate program back to the "local" setting (the classroom, the school, the community). We do not deny that exciting teaching and learning can sometimes occur in separate programs but, as discussed here, at a high social, financial, and emotional cost for all involved. Some of the most promising teaching strategies for the success of each student in integrated environments have derived from specialists in special education, gifted education, multicultural education, and reading who have discovered that their expertise can be used to the benefit of all students, not just a select few.

The lack of transfer from separate programs back to integrated environments results in students who fail when they return to integrated environments. For example, if some students thrive in smaller learning communities, then what can be done at the school to create such learning communities? If some students feel safer in separate settings, then what can schools do to ensure that all students feel safe? Moreover, educators learn that they, too, can succeed with a wide range of students, that success is not dependent on a few specialists who engage in some esoteric teaching "magic" with a few students. Indeed, nearly a decade ago, Newmann and Whelage (1995) learned in their study of separate programs for at-risk students that educators could provide all aspects of these programs in integrated environments.

Many well-meaning educators who are often advocates for students who struggle in school can become trapped in the enabling aspect of special programs. We were discussing with one school administrator the growing number of alternative schools in his part of the state. He agreed, "There is nothing that the alternative schools are doing that couldn't be done in the local high schools. But the high schools are not doing that, so we have to do something." We agree that "we have to do something" to meet the needs of students who are struggling in school. Simply to close down the alternative schools without changes in the local high school would not be fair to anyone involved. As long as the alternative schools or other separate programs exist, however, this situation provides little incentive for the schools to change to meet the needs of students of all abilities. We discuss in Chapter 14 ways educators can take a dual approach to change—that is, strive to meet the needs of students of all abilities now while working proactively on changes in the school such that these separate programs will not be necessary in the future.

The federal government has recognized the problems with separate programs in two ways. First, the reauthorization of the Individuals with Disabilities Act of 1997 states:

The education of children with disabilities can be made more effective by . . . coordinating this Act with other local, educational service agency, State, and Federal school improvement efforts in order to ensure that such children benefit from such efforts and *that special education can become a service for such children rather than a place where they are sent* [italics added].

Second, the Ed-Flex program allows schools the flexibility to provide services to students by using funding from Title I and other funding sources on a schoolwide basis in preventive ways (Robelen, 1999).

To avoid the problems of separate programs and to capitalize on these federal initiatives, schools must move from a program-based model to a service delivery model; that is, educators must provide services across children and environments in contrast with programs that are often set up specifically for a subgroup of children in a specific location.

When we meet the needs of students of all abilities by providing services rather than by establishing separate programs, we set the stage for a broad range of children to learn together, but even more so, we set the stage for a broad range of teachers to teach together. Thus we bring together teachers with a range of expertise to share their strengths related to good teaching (see Chapter 9). In so doing, we are better able to meet the needs of students who did not have their needs met in separate programs.

Now that we know the problems with program-based models and the advantages of providing services to students, in Chapter 2 we describe how schools and districts can move toward analyzing and determining the necessary steps to provide services.

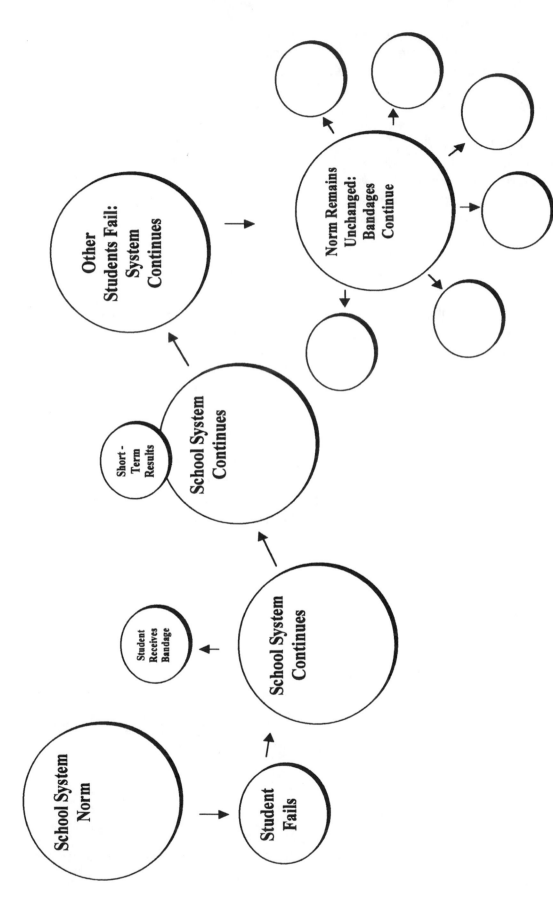

Colleen A. Capper, Elise Frattura, Maureen W. Keyes, *Meeting the Needs of Students of ALL Abilities: How Leaders Go Beyond Inclusion.*

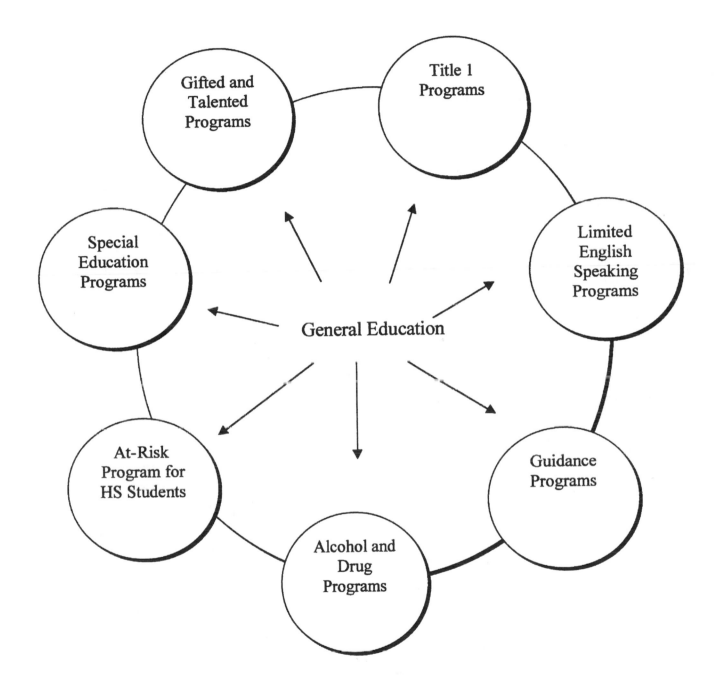

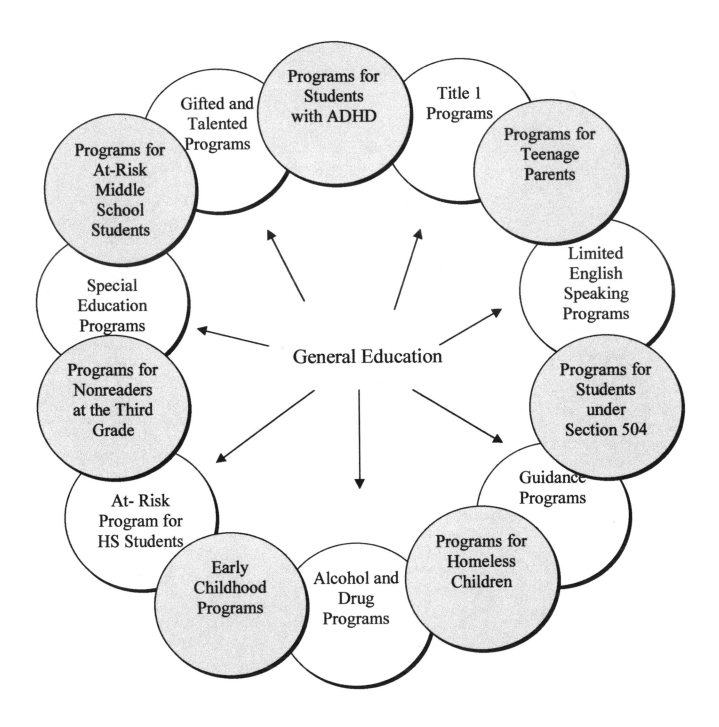

HANDOUT 1.4. Key Assumptions About Separate Programs

1. We can better serve students who struggle if they are separated from their peers.

2. We can only provide individual attention and support in a setting or situation separate from the student's peers.

3. Staff are incapable of teaching to a range of students.

4. Schools are incapable of changing to meet student needs.

5. The focus of student problems lies within the student; thus, we have no need to examine a student's history to determine how we might deliver services to avoid student struggle.

6. Students are more different than alike.

Colleen A. Capper, Elise Frattura, Maureen W. Keyes, *Meeting the Needs of Students of ALL Abilities: How Leaders Go Beyond Inclusion.* Copyright © 2000, Corwin Press, Inc.

HANDOUT 1.5. Eight Major Problems With Providing Separate Programs

1. Separate programs track and marginalize students of color and students of lower social classes.

2. Separate programs are costly.

3. Separate programs require personnel to expend a tremendous amount of resources in determining eligibility.

4. Separate programs result in some students receiving services and others being denied.

5. Separate programs fragment a student's day.

6. Separate programs blame and label students.

7. Separate programs enable educators and students not to change.

8. Separate programs prevent transfer of educator and student knowledge back to integrated environments.

HANDOUT 1.6. Cost Analysis of a Single Individual Evaluation*

Specialist	Assessment $/hr	Observation $/hr	Write-up $/hr	Meeting $/hr	Total
Psychologist	38.17(2)	38.17(2)	38.17(1.5)	38.17(3)	324.44
Special educator	38.17(2)	38.17(2)	38.17(1.5)	38.17(3)	324.44
Occupational therapist	38.17(2)	38.17(2)	38.17(1.5)	38.17(3)	324.44
Physical therapist	38.17(2)	38.17(2)	38.17(1.5)	38.17(3)	324.44
Speech and language	38.17(2)	38.17(2)	38.17(1.5)	38.17(3)	324.44
General educator	38.17(1)	38.17(2)	38.17(2)	38.17(2)	267.19
Administrator				40.28(3)	120.84
Other					
Total					2,010.23

NOTE: A district of 4,500 students averages 225 (5%) evaluations per year to total $443,713 per year.

*An average experienced teacher in the Midwest at master's + 15 credits on the salary scale receives $46,231 per year, with a $11,789 benefit package. Total salary for the teacher of $58,020 divided by 190 days, 8 hours per day, provides the reader with the hourly salary. An administrator's salary of $72,000 plus a benefits package of $11,789 for a total salary of $83,789 divided by 260 days, 8 hours per day, provides the reader with the hourly salary.

Self-Evaluation:
Leading Beyond Inclusion

Directions: Complete the following Likert-type scale by rating the level of success, as well as delineating strengths/ limitations, the next steps that should be taken, and what the timeline might look like.

5 = How we do business;   4 = Increased comfort level;   3 = Beginning implementation;
2 = Emerging through conversation;   1 = Yet to acknowledge as a need

Focus Area *Chapter 1: Services Rather Than Programs*	Likert-type Scale	Strengths/ Limitations	Next Steps	Timeline
Major area of emphasis:				
1. We are beginning to acknowledge the need for assessing how students receive services.	5 4 3 2 1			
2. We understand that programs are not cost-effective.	5 4 3 2 1			
3. We conduct an ongoing cost analysis of special programs in our school/district.	5 4 3 2 1			
4. We conduct ongoing cost analysis of evaluation and placement of students in special programs.	5 4 3 2 1			
5. We recognize that the eligibility requirements of programs require a tremendous amount of resources that could be used differently.	5 4 3 2 1			

		5 4 3 2 1		
6. We use what we have learned in special programs to improve education for each student in integrated environments.		5 4 3 2 1		
7. We acknowledge the negative consequences of labels.		5 4 3 2 1		
8. We agree that programs provide services to some but not to others.		5 4 3 2 1		
9. We acknowledge the ways separate programs can enable educators and students not to change.		5 4 3 2 1		
10. We acknowledge how university training can reinforce enabling and separate programs.		5 4 3 2 1		
11. We acknowledge the six assumptions of separate programs and the fallacies associated with these assumptions.		5 4 3 2 1		
12. We recognize the ways separate programs and student evaluations can fragment a student's day.		5 4 3 2 1		

Comments:

Colleen A. Capper, Elise Frattura, Maureen W. Keyes, *Meeting the Needs of Students of ALL Abilities: How Leaders Go Beyond Inclusion.*
Copyright © 2000, Corwin Press, Inc.

Chapter 2

First Stage

Ask Necessary Questions

For a school or district to move from a program delivery model to a service delivery model, we must analyze the current situation by asking necessary questions. These questions can prompt educators to evaluate why services are delivered as they currently are for each child, how services are delivered, who provides the services to whom, at what time services are provided, and where such services are delivered. In this chapter, we consider who asks the questions, how educators should ask these questions, and what questions we consider worth asking.

The person asking the questions can be anyone—a teacher, a building principal, the director of student services, a parent, a student, an instructional assistant, the superintendent. Meaningful change occurs when we can acknowledge questions that are worth asking and that anyone can ask. We must first feel comfortable asking and assisting others to ask questions about how schools function and then to listen to each other's words, keeping the child at the center of the conversation. In Handouts 2.1 and 2.2, we suggest questions that we believe are worth asking at both the district and school levels.

The questions, asked often and with sensitivity to people's experiences and feelings, will provoke conversation over time. When we invite questions from all, as the conversation unfolds we move from individual opinions to collective learning. That is, we move from the view that information is an asset we protect to the view that information is energy for a group; from privilege and power to collaboration; from performing to thinking and interacting; from directing to mentoring; from learned to learner; from problem driven to vision driven; from fragmentation to holism (Roberts, 1997). The intent is not to limit responding to the questions to an individual level but, rather, to elicit enough questions for building personnel to want to talk about how they provide a range of educational services across separately funded and legislated disciplines. Once the momentum from Stage 1 of moving toward service delivery—asking and responding to necessary questions—has risen to a level of genuine concern, educators can form a building team to examine service delivery for all students. Developing this team constitutes Stage 2 of moving from programs to services, and we discuss this in Chapter 3.

HANDOUT 2.1. Asking Necessary Questions at the Building Level

Sample Questions

1. What is the students' access to qualified teachers? _____
   _____
   _____

2. How are we ensuring that teachers and administrators who are hired are qualified to engage in successful teaching strategies for each student? _____
   _____
   _____

3. How is high-quality staff development being used to target student needs? _____
   _____

4. How and to what extent do teachers plan together? _____
   _____

5. How and to what extent do teachers have opportunities to observe, coach, and network with colleagues?
   _____

6. To what extent do we have partnerships with teacher preparation institutions? _____
   _____

7. What are our recruitment and induction practices? _____
   _____

8. To what extent do staff have opportunities for high-quality staff development? _____
   _____

9. What are our student-to-teacher ratios, and are they conducive to student learning? _____
   _____

10. How does the school climate support the success of each student? _____
    _____

11. Are teachers able to teach to a broad range of students? _____
12. Do teachers team within the grade level and across disciplines? _____
13. Are we successful with each student in integrated environments? _____
14. Could we better meet the needs of some of our struggling students? _____
15. Do students socialize across areas of needs? _____
16. Are some students required to leave their classrooms or schools (when others are not) to get their needs met? _____
17. How many students are currently bused who could potentially walk? _____
18. How will each student be successful with the academic standards? _____
    _____

19. Other: _____
    _____

20. Other: _____
    _____

SOURCE: Numbers 1-8 are adapted from Darling-Hammond and Falk (1997).

HANDOUT 2.2. Asking Necessary Questions at the District Level

Sample Questions	School 1	School 2	School 3	School 4	School 5
1. How are we ensuring that teachers and administrators who are hired are qualified to engage in successful teaching strategies for each student?					
2. What is students' access to qualified teachers?					
3. How is high-quality staff development being used to target student needs?					
4. How and to what extent do teachers plan together?					
5. How and to what extent do teachers have opportunities to observe, coach, and network with colleagues?					
6. Are students with all abilities and diversity currently attending their neighborhood school? If not, why not?					
7. Is anyone asking about how better to meet the needs of students? If so, who?					

(Continued)

Sample Questions	School 1	School 2	School 3	School 4	School 5
8. What is the district's mission statement? Is it in alignment with providing services versus programs?					
9. What do we value?					
10. How will we be successful with each student using a standards-based education?					
11. What is our expulsion rate? Why?					
12. What is our dropout rate? Why?					
13. Other					
14. Other					
15. Other					

SOURCE: Numbers 1-6 are adapted from Darling-Hammond and Falk (1997).

Self-Evaluation:
Leading Beyond Inclusion

Directions: Complete the following Likert-type scale by rating the level of success, as well as delineating strengths/limitations, the next steps that should be taken, and what the timeline might look like.

5 = How we do business;   4 = Increased comfort level;   3 = Beginning implementation;
2 = Emerging through conversation;   1 = Yet to acknowledge as a need

Focus Area *Chapter 2: Ask Necessary Questions*	*Likert-type Scale*	*Strengths/ Limitations*	*Next steps*	*Timeline*
Major area of emphasis:				
1. Questions are being asked and conversations are held about how services are implemented at the district level.	5 4 3 2 1			
2. Questions are being asked and conversations are held about how services are implemented at the building level.	5 4 3 2 1			
3. Other:	5 4 3 2 1			
4. Other:	5 4 3 2 1			

Comments:

Colleen A. Capper, Elise Frattura, Maureen W. Keyes, *Meeting the Needs of Students of ALL Abilities: How Leaders Go Beyond Inclusion.* Copyright © 2000, Corwin Press, Inc.

Chapter 3

Second Stage

Establish Teams to Respond to the Questions

The following 10 steps will assist you in developing a team of individuals to respond to the questions we suggested in Chapter 2 and to ask further questions (see Handout 3.1). In so doing, the teams can lay the groundwork for success for all students.

Step 1: How Should the Service Delivery Committee Evolve?

- Never force change. If you cannot generate enough interest at the building level or district level, continue to ask questions related to why you do what you do to serve all students. Are you meeting their needs the best way you know how?

- If enough individuals express interest and the momentum is strong, begin asking a range of individuals whether they would like to be part of a group to examine how better to meet the needs of all students.

- Keep the committee at the individual building level because each school has a range of different variables that those individuals delivering the service must discuss.

- A district-level committee should be formed to deal with district-level issues.

- Do not let the committee become a political platform regarding the merits of programs or models (e.g., ESL, gifted education, inclusion). Instead, the committee must serve as a place for informed discussion on the value of educating children together to meet their individual needs better.

Step 2: Who Should Serve as a Member of the Committee?

- The membership of the committee must be made up of a diverse range of disciplines and opinions around educational services. Do not exclude those with opinions that differ from those of others.

- The committee's membership should not be any larger than 8 to 10 individuals.

- The individuals should have strong opinions about the educational services offered all students.

- At the building level, the following representatives would be appropriate but not essential: two general educators, two special educators, a Title I or reading representative, the building principal, an instructional assistant, a parent, students (if age appropriate), a speech and language pathologist, an at-risk instructor, the director of student services, the director of curriculum and instruction, and the school psychologist.

- At the district level, the following representatives would be appropriate but not essential: a representative from each building team, the directors of instruction and student services, a school board member, and a parent.

Step 3: What Information Should the Group Receive as Reference Material?

- The collective intelligence of the group is essential; without appropriate supporting information, the group can function with collective ignorance that in the end will breed irreversible mistakes. The committee will require information regarding the following:

  a. Current data from the school and district about current programs and services (see Resource B for an example of data collection); committee members can collect baseline data at the school or district level and share this information with the team

    b. The cost of current services specific to the district, and public perspective regarding the cost of specialized services overall

    c. A copy of the district mission and charge for the year and future years

    d. Readings on why educators should include students with a range of needs (see reference list in Resource C as an example)

Step 4: Where to Begin?

- Set the ground rules. Allow the group to decide its own rules that it will abide by throughout the process.

- Allow time to discuss the readings by allowing each member to share his or her thoughts, hopes, and fears.

- Conduct the "Each Student Learns Best . . ." activity (described in the Introduction) with the committee.

- Conduct a gap analysis; that is, check the list of descriptors from the previous activity against the district mission statement and determine whether any descriptors disagree with the mission statement. If so, bring such a discussion to the district-level committee.

- Do not use budgetary reasons to limit the discussion of the descriptors.

Step 5: If Students Are Struggling in Our School/District, How Do We Currently Meet Their Needs?

- Have committee members use words or pictures or a combination to describe their current practices for students who are struggling.

- Ask members to list their practices that focus on preventing students from struggling and then compare this list to the description of practices for students who are struggling.

- Often, it is easier to have team members describe the formal programs by the following sections (see Handout 3.2 for a sample form): Intervention, Referral Process, Individual Assessment, Placement Procedures, Service Delivery Options, Budget Plans.

■ If you need other individuals not on the team to describe the services, invite those individuals to the meeting scheduled for this discussion or have other committee members meet with specific individuals to gather the data.

Step 6: How Do We Determine Where to Focus Our Energies?

■ Delineate those current services that agree with the list of descriptors of how each student learns best.

■ Delineate those current services that oppose the list of descriptors.

■ Discuss why the services are in opposition and some options for change.

■ Analyze why the services that are in alignment are successful and determine whether the service structure can be replicated (see Handout 3.3 for the spreadsheet to complete the analysis).

Step 7: How Do We Develop Our Service Delivery Model?

■ Begin without any budgetary concerns or limitations and draw or write how the services should look if they were to parallel the list of descriptors (see a sample in Handout 3.4).

■ Remember to keep what the committee has determined successful from the "Each Student Learns Best When . . ." activity.

Step 8: How Do We Share Our Progress With the Staff and Families?

■ Continue to update the staff and families of the committee's progress through 10-minute sound bites at staff meetings or service delivery news and in parent and staff news updates. Include why the committee formed, who is involved and why, how they will share information, and so on.

■ Make sure that staff and parents have the same data and information as the committee. In addition, it is important for the staff and families to understand that the charge of the committee is to create a service delivery model that meets the needs of each student in integrated educational settings.

■ Set a time for staff to offer responses to the committee regarding the recommended changes and ask for their insight and ideas. In addition, it may be appropriate to meet and have staff and families discuss their thoughts, hopes, and fears.

■ Staff should feel comfortable with the committee's formation and charge. If not, staff must ask more questions to raise awareness.

■ Complete a fist-to-five consensus activity (see the activity's description in the Introduction) about each proposed change to reach consensus.

Step 9: How Do We Determine When to Implement Services?

■ Begin any changes under a broad reform umbrella, rather than as "add-ons" to current practice. For example, do not create an "inclusion" or "multicultural" initiative. In addition, the goal should be *how* to teach diverse learners in integrated settings, not *whether* to do it.

■ Move methodically. Determine under each recommendation what needs to occur to allow for the successful implementation of each service.

■ Align the budget process.

■ Set the timeline based on resources and natural implementation breaks (e.g., summer recess, semester break). Again, look at a natural break or an umbrella to begin providing better services.

Step 10: What Do We Do About Our Budgetary Restrictions?

■ Recruit your business manager to help search for appropriate funding.

■ Merge funding resources to meet the needs of each child in integrated environments (see Chapter 13 on funding).

■ Aim for what you need and then creatively troubleshoot the funding issues.

The team process described in this chapter can be a lengthy one and will often take a committee about 18 to 24 hours of meeting time. In the end, they will have reached consensus on how to work proactively to provide better services to a range of students in integrated environments.

The committee must constantly bring back the discussion throughout Stage 1 and Stage 2 of moving from programs to services to how students are affected. For students to be successful, services must move from teacher centered to student centered. When students are successful, teachers are happier and more creative. When a school begins to shift from programs to services by asking necessary questions and by creating teams to address the questions, the roles of personnel will also begin to shift. In the next chapter, we discuss the ways the roles of personnel need to shift in schools that are successful for all children.

HANDOUT 3.1. Establish Teams to Respond to the Questions

Step 1:   How should the service delivery committee evolve?

Step 2:   Who should serve as a member of the committee?

Step 3:   What information should the group receive as reference material?

Step 4:   Where to begin?

Step 5:   If students are struggling in our school/district, how do we currently meet their needs?

Step 6:   How do we determine where to focus our energies?

Step 7:   How do we develop our service delivery model?

Step 8:   How do we share our progress with the staff and families?

Step 9:   How do we determine when to implement services?

Step 10:   What do we do about our budgetary restrictions?

Colleen A. Capper, Elise Frattura, Maureen W. Keyes, *Meeting the Needs of Students of ALL Abilities: How Leaders Go Beyond Inclusion.* Copyright © 2000, Corwin Press, Inc.

HANDOUT 3.2. Current Service Delivery Model

	Special Education	Section 504	Title I	Early Intervention	AODA	Psychology Services	Guidance Services	Social Work Services	ESL Services
Intervention									
Referral process									
Individual assessment									
Placement procedures									
Service delivery options									
Budget plans									

HANDOUT 3.3. Service Analysis Spreadsheet

Area of Focus	Services in opposition to descriptors delineating how students learn best	Services in alignment with descriptors delineating how students learn best	Service Recommendations
Intervention procedures			
Referral process			
Individual assessment			
Placement procedures			
Service delivery option			
Budget options			
Other information to consider			

HANDOUT 3.4. Drawing of a Future Service Delivery Model

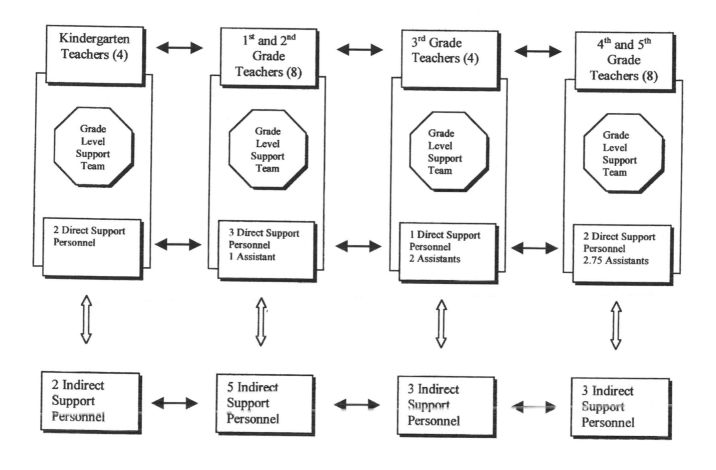

NOTES:

Each Support person is not assigned to more than one block to provide direct and indirect support.

Direct Support: May constitute current special educators, Title I support, instructional assistants, ESL, at-risk support.

Indirect Support: May constitute current guidance, social workers, building principal, psychologist, Title I, and so on.

SOURCE: Adapted from Sugar Creek Elementary School, Verona Wisconsin. Used with permission.

Colleen A. Capper, Elise Frattura, Maureen W. Keyes, *Meeting the Needs of Students of ALL Abilities: How Leaders Go Beyond Inclusion.* Copyright © 2000, Corwin Press, Inc.

Self-Evaluation:
Leading Beyond Inclusion

Directions: Complete the following Likert-type scale by rating the level of success, as well as delineating strengths/limitations, the next steps that should be taken, and what the timeline might look like.

5 = How we do business; 4 = Increased comfort level; 3 = Beginning implementation;
2 = Emerging through conversation; 1 = Yet to acknowledge as a need

Focus Area Chapter 3: Establish Teams to Respond to the Questions	Likert-type Scale	Strengths/ Limitations	Next Steps	Timeline
Major area of emphasis:				
1. A service delivery committee has evolved to respond to the questions.	5 4 3 2 1			
2. The team includes a representative sample of membership from the building or district of no more than 8 to 10 people.	5 4 3 2 1			
3. The team has collected and reviewed a range of reference materials and school and district data.	5 4 3 2 1			
4. The team has set up ground rules.	5 4 3 2 1			
5. The team has completed the "Each Student Learns Best When . . ." activity described in the Introduction.	5 4 3 2 1			

6. The team has completed a "gap analysis" comparing what works with the mission and practices.	5 4 3 2 1			
7. We have discussed the descriptors of our current services and displayed them in a visual or written format.	5 4 3 2 1			
8. We have determined where to focus our energies.	5 4 3 2 1			
9. The team has compared the current programs with the service delivery recommendations.	5 4 3 2 1			
10. A service delivery model is evolving to meet the range of learner needs better.	5 4 3 2 1			
11. We have communicated with staff and families about service delivery options.	5 4 3 2 1			
12. The implementation of a service delivery model begins methodically to meet the needs of all learners better.	5 4 3 2 1			
13. We creatively solve problems about budgetary issues.	5 4 3 2 1			

Comments:

Colleen A. Capper, Elise Frattura, Maureen W. Keyes, *Meeting the Needs of Students of ALL Abilities: How Leaders Go Beyond Inclusion.* Copyright © 2000, Corwin Press, Inc.

Chapter 4

Shift Personnel Roles to Meet Student Needs

If we choose to use the knowledge we have as an educational community about how students learn, then the roles of all educational personnel, from central office personnel to building principals to the cook's helper, must evolve to meet the changing needs of all students. Moving from providing programs for a few students to proactive services for all students requires educators who can work flexibly in a variety of settings with students who have diverse needs.

Villa and Thousand (1995) delineate responsibilities of educators within inclusive school communities. Although this delineation is helpful, in our work we have found that the descriptors are limited to a deficit model or an after-the-fact formation of inclusive programming. That is, this delineation assumes that general educators should provide services to the 70% to 80% of students perceived to be the norm. Special educators, ESL teachers, or at-risk specialists then provide adapted or modified services to students who may not meet the norm. In contrast, we assume that all educators are responsible for all students. Educators then develop instruction and services to meet student needs proactively and preventively rather than adapting the curriculum after a student fails.

To lead beyond inclusion, we must build the curriculum, instruction, and assessments from the ground up with a wide net of support for the range of learners and teachers. We must move beyond providing individualized education to the 20% to 30% of students who qualify for special education and other support programs to all students on the basis of how they learn and how they tell us what they know. Handout 4.1 identifies ways that educators' roles will shift. The handout includes the position title, traditional responsibilities, inclusive education responsibilities, and beyond inclusion responsibilities for each role.

HANDOUT 4.1. Shift Personnel Roles to Meet Student Needs: Leading Beyond Inclusion[1]

Position title	Traditional responsibilities	Inclusive education responsibilities	Beyond inclusion responsibilities
General education administrator	• Manages the general education program • Shifts responsibility for special programs to special education administrators, although special programs are "housed" within general education facilities	• Manages the educational programs for all students • Articulates the vision and provides emotional support to staff as they experience the change process • Participates as a member of collaborative problem-solving teams that invent solutions to barriers inhibiting the successful inclusion and education of any student • Secures resources to enable staff to meet the needs of all students	• Leads toward the merger of all services to wrap around all students based on needs • Builds the vision with the staff and provides emotional support to staff as their roles evolve to meet better the needs of all students • Participates as a member of collaborative problem-solving teams that invent solutions from the ground up in support of all students; does not wait for students to fail • Secures experienced staff to assist others in meeting the needs of all students • Secures resources to enable staff to meet the needs of all students
Teacher	• Refers students who do not "fit" into the traditional program for diagnosis, remediation, and possible removal • Teaches students who "fit" within the standard curriculum	• Shares responsibilities with special educators and other support personnel for teaching all assigned children • Seeks support of special educators and other support personnel for students experiencing difficulty in learning • Collaboratively plans and teaches with other members of the staff and community to meet the needs of all learners • Recruits and trains students to be tutors and social supports for one another	• Shares responsibilities with teachers with expertise in a range of areas to support all students • Creates a proactive preventative curriculum within climates that ensure student success • Works with educators who have a range of expertise to problem-solve around curriculum, climate, and social and behavioral supports to meet the needs of students experiencing difficulty in learning • Collaboratively plans and teaches with other members of the staff and community to meet the needs of all learners • Sets a classroom climate that assumes expectations of peer supports (students understand their role is to be supportive for each other in academic, social, and behavioral areas)
Special educator	• Provides instruction to students eligible for services in resource rooms, special classes, and special schools	• Collaborates with general educators and other support personnel to meet the needs of all learners • Team-teaches with regular educators in general education classes • Recruits and trains students to be peer tutors and social supports for one another	• No longer defined as a special educator, but a math, reading, behavioral, or instructional facilitator • Collaborates with all educators to develop curriculum and classroom climate to meet the needs of all learners • Shares responsibility for all students through teaming, individualized small-group instruction, and large-group instruction • Continues to model and support peer, academic, social, and behavioral mentoring

(Continued)

39

Position title	Traditional responsibilities	Inclusive education responsibilities	Beyond inclusion responsibilities
Psychologist	• Tests, diagnoses, assigns labels, and determines eligibility for students' admission to special programs	• Collaborates with teachers to define problems • Creatively designs interventions • Team-teaches • Provides social skills training to classes of students • Conducts authentic assessments • Trains students to be conflict mediators, peer tutors, and supports for one another • Offers counseling to students	• Collaborates with teachers to troubleshoot for the success of each student • Provides staff development for teachers to assist teachers in understanding human behavior and child development of even the most needy children • Collaboratively and creatively designs interventions • Shares teaching time in support of each student for psychological needs • Provides social skills training to classes of students • Conducts authentic and individualized assessments • Teaches students to be conflict mediators, peer tutors, and supports for students • Offers counseling to students
Support staff (e.g., physical therapist, occupational therapist, orientation and mobility specialist)	• Diagnoses, labels, and provides direct services to students in settings other than the classroom • Provides support only to students eligible for a particular special program	• Diagnoses, labels, and provides direct services to students at times in the classroom, but most of the time in settings other than the classroom • Provides support only to students eligible for a particular special program	• Is moving into grade-level support personnel for a specific percentage of time during the day • Is collaborating with other staff and exchanging information and teaching each other skills
Teaching assistant	• Works in segregated programs • If working in general education classrooms, stays in close proximity to, and works only with, students eligible for special services	• Provides services to a variety of students in general education settings • Facilitates natural peer supports within general education settings	• Provides services to a variety of students in individualized, small-group, and large-group instruction • Facilitates natural peer supports within all settings
Gifted and talented teacher	• Assesses and determines eligibility in the areas of academic, musical, arts, leadership, creativity, and so on for those students who excel in specific areas • Provides pull-out instruction for only those students who meet eligibility	• Usually has not been included in the inclusion of students with disabilities into general education environments • Provides services for those students eligible for gifted services by mentoring the general education teacher	• Moves into new roles that redefine her or his titles and responsibilities; staff become part of each educational team (e.g., grade-level support) either to provide services to a heterogeneous group of students or to work with teachers to build the curriculum from the ground up to meet better the range of learners in all educational situations
At risk	• Assesses and determines eligibility in the areas of truancy, academic success, delinquency, parent status, and so on • Provides pull-out instruction for only those students who meet eligibility	• Services for at-risk at the elementary level have been recipients of inclusive services by teachers better able to assist those students prior to a referral; however, at the secondary level services continue to be segregated by classrooms and/or buildings	• Moves into redefined titles and roles that provide services to a heterogeneous group of students or works with teachers to build the curriculum from the ground up to meet better the range of learners in all educational situations

Reading specialist	• Assesses and determines eligibility in reading • Provides pull-out instruction for only those students who meet eligibility	• Continues isolated services even when other students are receiving integrated reading support	• Works with all teachers to assist in the teaching of reading, as well as to provide individualized, small-group, and large-group instruction in the classroom
Director of student services	• Functions in isolation from other central office administration • Sets up categorical programs for students with disabilities and other needs • Assists in developing at-risk programs and/or schools • Completes mandatory state and federal reports	• Continues to function in isolation of other central office administration • Works with building principals to develop collaborative relationships between special and general educators • Continues to develop programs according to category, legislation, and funding mechanisms • Completes appropriate federal and state reports	• Shares role with other central office administrators in support of all students • Works with building principals to move from a program-based model that separates and segregates to a service delivery model that unifies support for all students • Continues to work with teams of educators to develop supports based on needs versus isolated funding mechanisms • Shares the responsibility across administrators in completing state and federal reports
Speech and language pathologist	• Assesses students for language and speech disorders • Sets up individualized and small-group instruction for students meeting eligibility • Pulls students out of general education on the basis of teacher schedules to meet the needs of 35 to 40 students	• Assesses students for language and speech disorders • Continues to set up individualized and small-group instruction for students meeting eligibility • Works within the general education classroom when appropriate to meet the language needs of a range of students	• Moves into new roles that redefine her or his titles and responsibilities; may become part of a grade-level team for a specific amount of time each day to a heterogeneous group of students or work with teachers to build the curriculum from the bottom up to meet better the range of learners in all educational situations
Guidance counselor	• Serves as a "gatekeeper to information about post-secondary and occupational opportunity" (Smith-Maddox & Wheelock, 1995, p. 224) • Steers students into academic tracks • Provides classroom guidance (often used by the general educator for prep time)	• Typically ignored in the inclusive literature • Role virtually does not change	• Assists families and teachers to provide services to students instead of slotting students into categorical programs • Works closely with building principal and other support staff to assist in synthesizing services to students • At the secondary level, orchestrates services and postsecondary options for all students • "...helps all students develop the knowledge to take advantage of future opportunities" (Smith-Maddox & Wheelock, 1995, p. 224) • Communicates high expectations for each student • Helps students link personal goals to high school plans • Motivates all students to pursue challenging course work

SOURCE: Adapted from *Creating an Inclusive School* by R. Villa and J. Thousand. Alexandria, VA: Association for Supervision and Curriculum Development. Copyright © 1995 by ASCD. Reprinted by permission. All rights reserved.

Colleen A. Capper, Elise Frattura, Maureen W. Keyes, *Meeting the Needs of Students of ALL Abilities: How Leaders Go Beyond Inclusion.* Copyright © 2000, Corwin Press, Inc.

Self-Evaluation:
Leading Beyond Inclusion

Directions: Complete the following Likert-type scale by rating the level of success, as well as delineating strengths/ limitations, the next steps that should be taken, and what the timeline might look like.

5 = How we do business; 4 = Increased comfort level; 3 = Beginning implementation; 2 = Emerging through conversation; 1 = Yet to acknowledge as a need

Focus Area *Chapter 4: Shift Personnel Roles to Meet Student Needs*	*Likert-type Scale*	*Strengths/ Limitations*	*Next Steps*	*Timeline*
Major area of emphasis:				
1. The current role of the administration can be described as • Traditional responsibilities • Inclusive education responsibilities • Beyond inclusion responsibilities	5 4 3 2 1 5 4 3 2 1 5 4 3 2 1			
2. The current role of teachers can be described as • Traditional responsibilities • Inclusive education responsibilities • Beyond inclusion responsibilities	5 4 3 2 1 5 4 3 2 1 5 4 3 2 1			
3. The current role of the school psychologist can be described as • Traditional responsibilities • Inclusive education responsibilities • Beyond inclusion responsibilities	5 4 3 2 1 5 4 3 2 1 5 4 3 2 1			
4. The current role of school support staff can be described as • Traditional responsibilities • Inclusive education responsibilities • Beyond inclusion responsibilities	5 4 3 2 1 5 4 3 2 1 5 4 3 2 1			
5. The current role of teaching assistants can be described as • Traditional responsibilities • Inclusive education responsibilities • Beyond inclusion responsibilities	5 4 3 2 1 5 4 3 2 1 5 4 3 2 1			

6. The current role of the gifted and talented teachers can be described as							
• Traditional responsibilities	5 4 3 2 1						
• Inclusive education responsibilities	5 4 3 2 1						
• Beyond inclusion responsibilities	5 4 3 2 1						
7. The current role of at-risk teachers can be described as							
• Traditional responsibilities	5 4 3 2 1						
• Inclusive education responsibilities	5 4 3 2 1						
• Beyond inclusion responsibilities	5 4 3 2 1						
8. The current role of reading specialists can be described as							
• Traditional responsibilities	5 4 3 2 1						
• Inclusive education responsibilities	5 4 3 2 1						
• Beyond inclusion responsibilities	5 4 3 2 1						
9. The current role of the director of student services can be described as							
• Traditional responsibilities	5 4 3 2 1						
• Inclusive education responsibilities	5 4 3 2 1						
• Beyond inclusion responsibilities	5 4 3 2 1						
10. The current role of the speech and language pathologist can be described as							
• Traditional responsibilities	5 4 3 2 1						
• Inclusive education responsibilities	5 4 3 2 1						
• Beyond inclusion responsibilities	5 4 3 2 1						
11. The current role of the school guidance counselor can be described as							
• Traditional responsibilities	5 4 3 2 1						
• Inclusive education responsibilities	5 4 3 2 1						
• Beyond inclusion responsibilities	5 4 3 2 1						

Comments:

Colleen A. Capper, Elise Frattura, Maureen W. Keyes, *Meeting the Needs of Students of ALL Abilities: How Leaders Go Beyond Inclusion.* Copyright © 2000, Corwin Press, Inc.

Chapter 5

Principals Must Ensure Student Success

In previous work, we reviewed and analyzed three related strands of literature: (a) the principal's role in inclusive schools, (b) the principal's role in school reform, and (c) democratic and empowering principals. In this chapter, we join these three strands. On the basis of our previous analyses, we articulate 11 practical strategies for school principals in cocreating schools for the success of all students (see Handout 5.1; see also Capper, Theoharis, & Keyes, 1998, for additional literature citations to support these strategies):

Strategy 1: Cocreate and Sustain a Nonnegotiable Vision

Despite personal beliefs, educators using the exercise "Each Student Learns Best When . . .," described in the Introduction, can usually agree on what students need to be successful. Using this process, principals can collaboratively mix their beliefs with those of other educators and create a common purpose. The notion that each student is entitled to a quality education with other students, however, is not negotiable. These principals openly discuss their commitment to the success of all students despite possible contention and dissent.

Having a strong nonnegotiable vision that each student belongs focuses the principal's work and makes the principal more accountable to his or her vision. Simply claiming goals such as "improving achievement for all children" or "success for all" is not enough unless the principal is specific about which students to whom he or she is referring. The principal needs to make clear that *all* students are a part of this vision, including those students whom educators typically ignore in school reform, such as students with severe disabilities or those with challenging behaviors, gay/lesbian students, or students who, because of appearance, style of clothes, or intellectual abilities, do not fit in.

While holding to the belonging vision, principals must make high achievement for all students a priority. Newmann and Whelage (1995) concur, saying, "The recent education reform movement gives too much attention to changes in school organization that do not directly address the quality of student learning" (p. 51). As such, principals could successfully include all students, restructure their schools, or empower teachers with no measurable difference in student learning outcomes. Principals cannot allow this to happen.

Holding both goals—achievement and belonging—in high priority can also serve as a political strategy. This strategy reminds parents and the community that the principal will not allow student achievement to suffer by including each student, and that high student achievement in all domains—academic and social—can only be achieved in schools that are supportive of all students.

Strategy 2: Lead by Example

At the outset, most principals publicly articulate their personal commitment to addressing the needs of each student in an environment of high expectations where all students belong. Then, these principals model involvement and acceptance for each student. The principals' modeling creates a positive climate within the school for each student. These principals express a "we can do it" attitude and enthusiasm that permeate staff and student interactions.

To provide a positive example to other educators, these principals do not espouse a community where each student is valued and then take actions to contradict their views. For example, they seek proactive ways to educate students who have challenging behaviors without resorting to expulsion (see Chapter 11). They do not advocate to support all students and then seek to establish separate "at-risk" programs (e.g., schools-within-schools, charter schools, alternative schools) no matter how benevolent these efforts might seem.

Strategy 3: Cocreate an Implementation Plan

Most principals develop systematic plans that incorporate how to ensure that success for each student will happen, whether the plan has a voluntary or mandatory scope, and what they as a school will and will not do (Louis & Miles, 1990). These principals develop strategies to institute high achievement practices that value each student by adopting either a slow or a more accelerated implementation plan, depending on district circumstances. They build the first method upon the efforts of two or three teacher volunteers. Staff and students begin to learn about belonging and high achievement and slowly change as those pioneering the effort demonstrate these practices in their classrooms. This slow start provides time for staff to become familiar with these practices and lessens teachers' fears.

A few principals immediately carry out these changes for the entire school. This implementation, accompanied by many supporting efforts, pushes the whole building into involvement with caring, high-expectation schools: learning, developing, and problem-solving together. These principals often work in large school districts that support these practices. Staff who are unwilling to work with the school's vision either retire or transfer to other schools in the district.

Despite implementation style, successful principals create task forces or committees to study and monitor the implementation process (see Chapter 3). These collaborative groups, which include teachers, parents, and sometime students, study and learn more about various aspects of service delivery. Task force meetings often result in policies stating that all staff are responsible for all students and that the school is committed to a quality education for each student. The principals' active involvement in the planning and implementation processes is essential to the successful implementation of these practices.

Strategy 4: Lead Collaboratively/ Develop Trust

Although successful principals for all students maintain a "bottom line" about the goal of high-achievement practices in a context of belonging, they empower staff, parents, the community, and students to participate in all decisions to reach that goal. Janney, Snell, Beers, and Raynes (1995) interviewed staff at 10 schools and quoted one principal's advice: "Rather than informing staff 'we're going to do this,' [g]et information yourself and share ideas with staff, ask how this can work in our school" (p. 433). Successful principals of all students form work groups, develop leadership teams, invest in staff facilitators, and share authority as ways to provide opportunities for staff to take part in collaborative decision making (Fullan, 1985). These collaborative strategies cultivate trust among participants that is central to successful implementation.

With their collaborative efforts, principals need to keep their vision clear. Although at times work toward the vision may derive from collective reflection, at other times specific change is urgent. Both require collaborative skills to bring the vision to fruition.

Strategy 5:
Recruit Teacher Volunteers but Maintain the Goal of All Students, All Staff

As previously mentioned, principals often solicit teacher volunteers to operationalize their vision of success for each student. Hines and Johnston (1996) advocate for recruiting the teachers who are most flexible and most comfortable with ambiguity.

In the Janney et al. study (1995), interviewees described their satisfaction with the self-nomination process and reported this as the "best way to encourage more teachers to become involved" (p. 433). Interviewed teachers in a study by Keyes (1996) reported knowing their principal's stated goal, yet also knowing that those of them who felt unsure about their skills in this area would have more time to develop.

Not only does soliciting teacher volunteers decrease teacher resistance, but this action also sows the seeds for future success. For example, one principal stated, "Teachers here have seen the successes and want to be part of it. Everyone looks on and says, 'I'd love to be able to . . . have those successes' " (Janney et al., 1995, p. 433). Teachers report a sense of relief knowing that they will be able to learn from the advance work of their colleagues who volunteer. Some principals facilitate initial planning meetings with teacher volunteers, often the summer before implementation (Keyes, 1996; Lutz, 1994).

When taking incremental steps toward high-achieving schools where all students respect and honor each other, principals must not lose sight of the ultimate goal: each student included and high-achieving, all staff involved. One mistake that principals may make is to reach one goal and then, because of the effort it took to reach that goal, decide to pursue no further. For example, some principals begin this work by including students with labels together in one or two classrooms, which is termed *clustering*. They argue that staff can better serve students if the students with labels are clustered in one or two classrooms at one grade level rather than dispersed in natural proportions across classrooms (e.g., no more than 10%-12% of students in one class with special needs or a special education label). Indeed, principals may use clustering as one step toward including students in natural proportions, but they need to make clear that this practice is temporary until they can strategize how to include students equitably across all classrooms.

Strategy 6: Be Visible, Accessible, Approachable, and Involved

As the previous strategies mention, being visible, accessible, approachable, and involved encourages educators to share their views and to work through their fears. Principals who strive for the success of all students make it a point to understand what is going on in every grade and every classroom. These principals work on a daily basis with students and staff to foster the importance of critical thought and at the same time work with staff to look critically at what they do and why they do it (Reitzug, 1994).

Strategy 7: Encourage and Support Risk Taking

Principals of schools that are successful for all students create a risk-free, safe school climate where they will not criticize teachers for trying new teaching strategies (Reitzug, 1994). They encourage teachers to try new ideas and to make mistakes. This approach leads to the development of an atmosphere of critique in which educators couple thoughtful reflection with risk taking (Reitzug, 1994). One teacher remarked, "[The principal] lets us know that [we] might try something that might not work and it [would] be okay" (Allen, 1995, pp. 142-143).

Strategy 8: Confront Challenges With Action Research

Principals who work toward the success of all students do not shy away from the challenges of this work. They use action research as one way to confront problems and challenges with staff, students, and parents. They understand the value of inquiry-oriented action wherein staff reflect on and examine their daily practices (Reitzug, 1994).

These principals also help teachers conduct their own action research projects. Educators can use action research for making instructional and curricular decisions to meet the diverse range of student needs in the classroom (Anderson, Herr, & Nihlen, 1994). Data for this research are collected from traditional sources (attendance records, grades, test scores), conventional sources (surveys, interviews), and creative sources (student portfolios, demonstrations of student learning, videotapes, exhibits) (Blase, Blase, Anderson, & Dungan, 1995). Being successful with all students is more likely to be institutionalized if principals coordinate a persistent effort to create and problem-solve via action research.

Strategy 9: Hire Compatible Staff

In collaboration with teachers, parents, and community members, principals hire staff as a way to strengthen their core beliefs and vision. These principals commit themselves to having only quality teachers on staff (Mizell, 1995), with *quality* defined, in part, as (a) teachers willing to work with a diverse range of students in the classroom and (b) teachers with the requisite skills to teach diverse students successfully or the willingness to learn those skills. When filling vacancies, these principals hire faculty who meet these quality criteria. Hiring conveys an important symbolic message as it reflects the kinds of values desired at the school. Hiring compatible staff is also a practical way of gaining teachers who share the new vision and who can be an active part of the school's community. In the long term, this hiring strategy decreases the need for "baseline" staff development (Morgan & Demchak, 1996). These principals help teachers enhance or change their professional performance and replace those who do not or cannot change (Benoy, 1996).

Strategy 10: Support Staff

Principals who are successful with each student play an active role in finding ways to make it easier for their teachers to do their jobs according to the vision of the school. They provide four kinds of staff support: (a) general, ongoing support; (b) staff development; (c) time and scheduling support; and (d) resources and materials.

General, Ongoing Support

Principals who are successful with each student develop supportive climates by articulating, modeling, reinforcing, promoting, and providing structures that support the development of high achievement where each student believes that he or she is an integral member of the school community.

Such principals stress the importance of collaborative teaching and other mechanisms that self-perpetuate ongoing support for teachers during the school year and the following years. They also foster cooperative and consultative teaching models by matching teachers with compatible partners. As mentioned previously, the principals also provide ongoing support by encouraging teachers to be risk takers and not to expect perfection from themselves or each other.

Staff Development

Successful principals engage their staff in professional learning that supports schoolwide change. These principals, however, do allow staff development to emerge from teacher needs and to evolve naturally as part of their classroom action research. In this context, they make professional learning a priority for their teachers and for themselves. For some principals, staff development can be the first component in moving toward change (Ellis, 1996). They also use staff development as a means to integrate new teachers into the culture and to build their capacity for reform as well (Mizell, 1995). This learning is not one-time education but, rather, an ongoing commitment to building their organization.

Successful principals of each student insist that all staff, including custodial, secretarial, and other support staff, are involved in staff development. An all-encompassing staff development is vital because if children are to be successful within the entire school community, then all staff members working in the school are responsible for helping make this happen.

Time and Scheduling Support

School principals who are successful with each student construct schedules to provide time and opportunity for meetings among teachers. Providing flexibility in scheduling allows teachers to work together to develop a proactive and creative curriculum, instruction, and classroom climate that prevents student struggles. These meetings can also help teachers develop creative ideas for student struggles (Rankin, 1995).

Successful principals also develop heterogeneous class lists to reflect the population of the school (Allen, 1995); that is, principals assign each student to a grade or homeroom. Moreover, students are not tracked into homerooms, classrooms, or courses on the basis of their perceived abilities (no more than 10%-12% of students in one class are labeled with a disability), and all courses reflect the gender, race/ethnicity, and social class demographics of the school. No class has a disproportional number of students of color, male or female students, or students receiving free or reduced-price lunches.

Resources and Materials

Successful principals provide tangible support in resources, teaching materials, literature and information, classroom space, competent paraprofessionals, and money and release time for planning sessions and staff development. They find ways to see to it that teachers have what they need to do their jobs. This commitment to the fact that teachers need certain resources adds to the climate of empowerment by viewing and portraying teachers as professionals (Reitzug, 1994).

Teachers and students benefit from the distribution of resources. Principals allocate these resources in ways that are consistent with meeting the needs of students of all abilities (Murphy, 1994). Teachers team together to use the resources they have in creative and flexible ways (McKee, 1997). Successful principals find ways to provide the needed resources (human, material, and financial) to support each student, even in times of scarcity.

Creating and sustaining schools that are successful for each student requires a necessary flow of information. Principals who are successful with each student provide necessary information to the staff to make shared decision making work (O'Hair & Reitzug, 1997). This flow helps keep everyone up to date about day-to-day activities and larger issues. Principals use their own action research, school and district data, and published research as a basis for knowledge and planning (Benoy, 1996). They provide articles and information about professional development opportunities. This professional information encourages critique and reflective practice on being successful with a range of students (Reitzug, 1994). In addition, these principals encourage and include diverse and previously excluded perspectives (via people or literature), which in turn provides new information.

Strategy 11: Take Strategic Action With Parents and the Community

As principals encourage the gathering and distributing of information, ideas, and resources with their staffs, they also play that same role with parents and the community. Parent and community education is an activity that helps create schools that are successful with all students. Meeting with parents and community members to address concerns and to solicit suggestions counters parental fears (Lutz, 1994).

Successful principals encourage the entire staff to act as a balancer between the school and the community. Sharing information about how all students can belong and succeed helps parents, the community, and the school district understand what is happening within the school and builds support for school change.

Successful principals also find ways to use the resources and expertise of parents, businesses, universities, health and human services, and community organizations (Newmann & Whelage, 1995) to meet the needs of students of all abilities. This strategic involvement not only adds to the resource and knowledge base of the school but also encourages parents and community members to be actively involved to meet the needs of each student.

In sum, the principal must engage in many important strategies for the success of each student. Principals need to help build a collective, nonnegotiable vision; lead by example; cocreate an implementation plan; lead collaboratively, which nurtures trust; recruit teacher volunteers while maintaining the goal of all staff being successful with each student; be visible and involved; encourage risk taking; value and use action research; hire and support compatible staff; and strategically work with parents and the community. They also must be creative with funding, which we discuss in Chapter 13. On the basis of our extensive review of the literature and what works in the field, we agree that principals who are successful with each student focus their vision and practice to the heart of education—high student achievement for each student that takes place in a school community that values and respects each student. Principals can also be greatly supported in their efforts to ensure student success if they work collaboratively with the central office administration. We take this up in Chapter 6.

HANDOUT 5.1. Principals Must Ensure Student Success

Strategy 1: Cocreate and sustain a nonnegotiable vision.

Strategy 2: Lead by example.

Strategy 3: Cocreate an implementation plan.

Strategy 4: Lead collaboratively/develop trust.

Strategy 5: Recruit teacher volunteers but maintain the goal
of all students, all staff.

Strategy 6: Be visible, accessible, approachable, and involved.

Strategy 7: Encourage and support risk taking.

Strategy 8: Confront challenges with action research.

Strategy 9: Hire compatible staff.

Strategy 10: Support staff.

Strategy 11: Take strategic action with parents and the community.

Self-Evaluation:
Leading Beyond Inclusion

Directions: Complete the following Likert-type scale by rating the level of success, as well as delineating strengths/limitations, the next steps that should be taken, and what the timeline might look like.

5 = How we do business; 4 = Increased comfort level; 3 = Beginning implementation;
2 = Emerging through conversation; 1 = Yet to acknowledge as a need

Focus Area Chapter 5: Principals Must Ensure Student Success	Likert-type Scale	Strengths/ Limitations	Next Steps	Timeline
Major area of emphasis:				
1. Our principals cocreate and sustain a nonnegotiable vision.	5 4 3 2 1			
2. Our principals lead by example.	5 4 3 2 1			
3. Our principals cocreate implementation plans.	5 4 3 2 1			
4. Our principals lead collaboratively and develop trust.	5 4 3 2 1			
5. Our principals recruit teacher volunteers but maintain the goal of all students, all staff in meeting the needs of students of all abilities.	5 4 3 2 1			
6. Our principals are visible, accessible, approachable, and involved.	5 4 3 2 1			

7. Our principals encourage and support risk taking.	5 4 3 2 1	
8. Our principals confront challenges with action research.	5 4 3 2 1	
9. Our principals hire compatible staff.	5 4 3 2 1	
10. Our principals support staff by providing • general/ongoing support • staff development for all personnel • staff development tied directly to instruction • time to collaborate and flexible scheduling • resources and materials	5 4 3 2 1 5 4 3 2 1 5 4 3 2 1 5 4 3 2 1 5 4 3 2 1	
11. Our principals take strategic action with parents and the community.	5 4 3 2 1	
12. Our principals work holistically and collaboratively with central office administrators.	5 4 3 2 1	

Comments:

Colleen A. Capper, Elise Frattura, Maureen W. Keyes, *Meeting the Needs of Students of ALL Abilities: How Leaders Go Beyond Inclusion.* Copyright © 2000, Corwin Press, Inc.

Chapter 6

The Central Office Must Walk the Talk

The exhilarating, contagious, and inspirational transformation of roles and responsibilities of educators toward the goal of creating and sustaining schools that work for each student must include the central office. The momentum, however, usually stops there. Disciplinary silos (e.g., student services, curriculum and instruction, business services) remain the central structure of the administrative office in most school systems. Districtwide administrators are often the facilitators of change, the leaders of growth for everyone but themselves. When we seek to cocreate schools that are successful for each student, maintaining the balkanization of central office staff becomes a destructive practice.

According to Quinn (1996), real change can only exist in systems when every level is part of that change process:

> I once worked with a top management team of a very large company. . . . In an effort to improve their organization, they had decided to send all the senior people to a well-known seminar on quality. These executives, upon returning from the enlightening seminar, decided to implement the ideas in their organization. Together they developed a reasonable plan and initiated the change effort. . . . Upon hearing their comments, I shared with them a story that was told to me by a vice-president at another company. . . . They also anticipated that their new plan would yield dramatic improvements in quality, morale, productivity, and profit. However, three years later, they found that their immense effort had little, if any impact. . . . "Why did it fail?" . . . [O]ne of the most influential members of the group said, "The leaders of the company didn't change their behavior." I nodded and pointed out that they themselves had made a lot of assumptions about the behavior that was going to change in others. Now I challenge them: "Identify one time when one of you said that you were going to change your behavior." (p. 101)

Quinn (1996) emphasizes the importance of understanding the incongruity of central office administrators asking for change in others while failing to exhibit the same level of commitment in themselves. Within the public school system, change generally comes from either a top-down or a bottom-up site-based decision process; either way, central office administrators seldom engage in deep, fundamental change.

The appointment of new superintendents usually results in some organizational change, typically with alterations in the administrative organizational chart. However, administrators do not spend time exploring the potential for deep change within the administrative structure that can support and model the changes expected of administrators and other educators at the building level.

According to Quinn (1996), "We cannot easily recognize that the problem is part of the system in which we play an active role. Our first inclination is always from a perspective that externalizes the problem, keeps it somewhere 'out there' " (p. 102). When central office staff believe that the problem is "out there," the onus for problem resolution is "out there" as well. We impede systemic change throughout the district when we do not include the central office in the shift of problem ownership. If the district believes in creating a community of learners that embraces high expectations within a context of belonging, then the full participation of central office staff as students of learning becomes imperative.

Traditional Roles of Central Office Administrators Impede Change

In the mid-1980s, researchers attempting to predict the needs of public schools thought that increased role specialization within the central administrative office would require the hiring of various specialty consultants in areas such as mathematics, learning disabilities, or computer technology (Campbell, Cunningham, Nystrand, & Usdan, 1985). Campbell et al. suggested the building of more specialization silos within each discipline. In the early 1990s, Lunenburg and Ornstein (1991) described what many school personnel were discovering: The role of the building principal had transformed from that of a building manager to a leader for all kinds of educational endeavors across many disciplines during and outside typical school hours.

In contrast, most central office staff roles across the country are currently formed under the following five specializations or silos (see Handout 6.1):

1. *Student services:* those services considered adjunct to curriculum, including special education, at-risk, alcohol and other drug abuse programs (AODA), and Title I

2. *Curriculum and instruction:* those services that are about curriculum, including subject areas, student data, and standards/benchmarks

3. *Business services:* those services that revolve around the financial stability of the schools

4. *Human resources/Personnel:* those services in support of staff needs throughout the district

5. *District administrator:* reports directly to the school board and administrative team to orchestrate services districtwide

For too long, such ways of organizing school structures have impeded school leaders from developing a unified system of services for all students across the district. In most school districts across the country, these positions function as separate entities from each other as they attempt to support the district as a whole. Central office administrators often satisfy requests for their services from building-level educators in fragmented and knee-jerk ways—typical of schools operating from traditional models (see Handout 6.2). This "expert-on-call" model continues within districts that have refused to develop more proactive, integrated, decentralized structures.

The expert-on-call model often prohibits staff members themselves from learning to problem-solve. It also prevents them from taking ownership of the situation and having confidence in themselves to know how to take proactive action.

With deep change, central office leaders do not maintain their traditional titles or remain in their distinct offices while initiating dialogue among district educators toward substantive change. Admittedly, change can be difficult for most people. The more entrenched one's knowledge base and comfort level, the more difficult change is, including change for central office administrators. Many fears continue to perpetuate the need for central office administrators to function from the protected silo model. In a survey in Milwaukee County (Wisconsin), administrators cited six reasons for perpetuating the centralized service delivery model: (a) lack of preparation; (b) certification and license parameters, especially those of student services directors; (c) past experiences; (d) structural constraints; (e) the current K-12 model; and (f) the sense that the breadth of information required by one person to do the job well was excessive.

Ironically, students are leading the need for all staff, including administrators, to change—beyond the surface, beyond cosmetic—in support of the whole learner. Our learners are telling us that they need us to put our heads together and wrap a unified system around them.

Transforming From Centralized Leaders to Stewards in Support of Learning

We have identified three stages that can move the central office toward roles and responsibilities that create and sustain schools successful with each student: (a) inquiry analysis, (b) role analysis, and (c) merging roles.

Stage 1: Inquiry Analysis

The transformation of the central office administration must begin with inquiries to help in defining the issue. The *inquiry analysis* is a process used to define the need for change and to determine necessary reconstructive techniques to move along a continuum toward deep change. One response may elicit another question, and as we pose and respond to questions, we generate thoughts toward reconstruction and transformation. As the general discourse occurs, the sharing of information shapes to future direction. Participants in the conversation may be central office only, or all administration, or a representative group of administrators, teachers, parents, school board members, and students. Initially, however, beginning with a small group may be best, and gradually adding others to the group process while sharing earlier accomplishments of the group. The comfort level of all participants is essential, but especially for those whose roles are being redefined.

The initial question in the inquiry analysis could be "How do we define an administrative leader?" Additional questions include "Are we where we want to be with our leadership?" and "How are central office services aligned with the district's vision and mission statement?" (A list of questions for an inquiry analysis process for a central office leadership team is included in Handout 6.3.)

During this process, central office staff could benefit from learning about conceptions of leadership that move beyond traditional ideas. For example, Greenleaf (1991) depicts a leader as a servant to the people built on relationships rooted in community. Successful leaders embody their group's most precious values and beliefs. These leaders persist and deepen as they learn to use life's wounds to discover their own spiritual centers. As they make peace with their demons within, they achieve the inner peace and bedrock confidence that enable them to inspire others.

Central office administrators can take a stewardship approach to leading and spend more time listening and asking questions. Taking a stewardship approach to leading may be easier for building principals than for central office administrators. Often, central office administrators have allowed politics and prestige to take over their reason for leading. As stewards to the district, central office administrators will find their roles evolving in support of all students. In sum, stewardship is an essential ingredient for leading to meet the needs of students of all abilities.

Stage 2: Role Analysis

The formal structure of schools includes the roles and responsibilities of central office staff. The formal structural component includes the actual parameters of administrators' roles, the person(s) to whom they report, and how they spend their day. Each central office staff member should analyze her or his current job and document her or his work tasks into three categories: (a) management, (b) reactionary leadership, and (c) proactive stewardship. In completing this analysis, administrators often have a better perspective on how they spend their time (see Handout 6.4 for an example of a student services director job analysis). In the example in Handout 6.4, the student services director clearly spends a significant amount of time in the reactionary leadership phase troubleshooting situations that were not initially set up in support of each student (e.g., curriculum, technology, assessment). Often, administrators also become mired in regulations and compliance. We have found that when educators possess a strong, practical understanding of the law and requirements, they can move beyond compliance toward proactive leadership. The proactive stewardship column should include a range of activities that, once underway, will help decrease the activities listed in the reactionary leadership column. The administrator should strive to engage in proactive stewardship approximately 70% of the time, reactionary leadership 20% of the time, and management 10% of the time.

Once each central office administrator has completed her or his job analysis, the administrators can examine where overlap occurs in their roles and where they might collaborate in their work (see Handout 6.5). The goal of the targeted collaborative tasks is to decrease the time spent on reactionary activities.

Stage 3: Merging Roles

Moving out of disciplinary silos in the central office remains a large task. For any change to be successful, the change should start small, at a level that is comfortable for all. At the central administration level, merging roles and responsibilities can occur for specific agendas, initiatives, reports, or other sequential/concrete tasks they must accomplish (Handout 6.6). For example, on completion of an analysis between the student services director and the curriculum and instruction director, two or three primary areas might emerge for which they can share ownership, such as diversity issues, standards, or assessment. In one school district, the student services director presented information to the school board about developing curriculum standards and benchmarks in the district—a presentation that traditionally would have been the responsibility of the curriculum and instruction director. Similarly, the curriculum and instruction director in another district conducted workshops with staff developing alternative assessments for students with severe disabilities.

Over time, a new role for these two distinct administrative positions can evolve into a merger of curriculum and support services, with one possible title being teaching and learning facilitator (see Handout 6.7, which shows traditional position descriptions and a joint position description for a teaching and learning facilitator). Given the breadth and depth of the work involved in both positions, merging the positions would require maintaining the current number of personnel in such positions. We could divide this new position between buildings or sections of the district, however, to provide more comprehensive services or divide by grade level (an elementary facilitator for teaching and learning and a secondary facilitator for teaching and learning, as depicted in Handout 6.8). In short, we can merge the tasks typically delineated for the curriculum and instruction director and the student services director to support all students. The teaching and learning facilitator then provides services to schools for all students, building the curriculum from the ground up and developing standards and benchmarks to encompass the range of learning attributes across all student abilities in the district.

The remaining central office roles may continue to function in specific areas, such as business services or personnel, but it is essential that the role of reactionary leader in these positions be dissolved to one of proactive steward for all students. For example, the business manager must merge funding sources rather than maintain separate funding categories among programs. Traditionally, business managers base financial decisions on legal parameters that can drive reactionary program delivery models—models that segregate students by need or abilities.

In a restructured central office that emphasizes stewardship to each student, the human resource or personnel director can be responsible for helping schools secure professionals who are successful with a range of students. In this way, central office educators are modeling the transformation from segregated programs to those that bring services to all students across the district.

A central office administration that views itself as steward to each student in the district is one of four cornerstones of deep change in the district. The other three cornerstones are (a) a district vision and mission that support the learning of each student; (b) a committed staff, including teachers responsible for teaching the entire range of students; and (c) building principals dedicated to high achievement paired with an emphasis on belonging and community. When the participants agree with these cornerstones, then the real work can begin; central office administrators must model the way.

No longer can the central office function under a model of administrative convenience—that is, that it provides services to students on the basis of convenience for administrators. When central office administrators begin to merge roles and services to the schools, they symbolically and practically model that all staff must provide an array of services to meet student needs. When we can capture this merged sense of responsibility across professional disciplines, a system of responsive schools that meet the needs of all students will have truly evolved.

HANDOUT 6.1. Traditional Roles of Central Office Administrators

Student Services	Curriculum and Instruction	Business Services	Human Resources/ Personnel	District Administrator
• Policy about discrimination needs • Grant writing • Guidance and counseling • Student assistance and AODA • School-age parents (SAP) • Tuition requests • School social work • School psychologist • Screening for special education and early entrance • At-risk programs • Health and nursing services • Student records • ESL services • Gifted and talented services • Special education summer programs • Exceptional educational programs • OT and PT services • Special transportation	• C & I Committee • All K-12 curriculum areas • Library programming • Media services • Summer school • Staff development • Textbook selection • Title I • Student trips • Program evaluation • Standards and assessment	• Facilities and finance • Audit • Financing • Purchasing • Insurance • Employee benefits • Payroll • Inventory • School lunch • Negotiation statistics • Contracted services • Property purchase • Investments • Building rentals • Temporary and long-term employees • Accounts payable • Loans • Energy management • Maintenance • Custodial • Budget planning • Accounting • Warehousing and internal delivery system	• Personnel committee • Recruiting • Employment • Salary administration • Employee evaluation • Labor relations • Contract administration • Grievance and mediation • Noncertified employees • Employee discipline • Employee assistance • Employee recognition • School staffing • Substitute staff • Student teachers	• Collaboration with school board • Oversight of all administrative positions • Public relations • Formation of broad picture

SOURCE: Adapted from School District of Waukesha [Wisconsin] (1993). Used with permission.

Colleen A. Capper, Elise Frattura, Maureen W. Keyes, *Meeting the Needs of Students of ALL Abilities: How Leaders Go Beyond Inclusion.* Copyright © 2000, Corwin Press, Inc.

HANDOUT 6.2. Traditional Central Office Structure

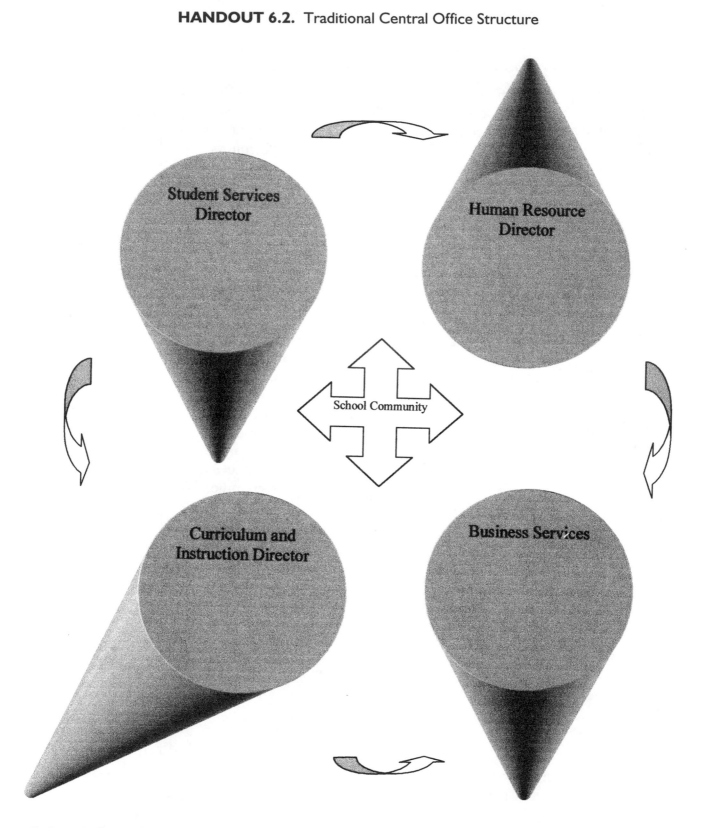

HANDOUT 6.3. Necessary Questions for Central Office Administrators

Inquiry	Current Structure	Where We Want to Be
1. How do we define administrative leadership?		
2. Are we where we want to be with our leadership?		
3. How are educational services aligned with the district vision and mission statement?		
4. What is the role of central office administration with each student?		
5. What is the role of central office administration with building principals?		
6. What is the role of central office administration with teaching and support staff?		
7. What is the role of central office administration as the keeper of the vision/ mission statement?		
8. What is the role of central office administration with and across other central office administrators?		
9. What is the role of central office administration with the school board?		
10. Is the role of central office administration different from that of the building principals?		
11. How do we see our roles unfolding over the next 5 years? 10 years?		

Colleen A. Capper, Elise Frattura, Maureen W. Keyes, *Meeting the Needs of Students of ALL Abilities: How Leaders Go Beyond Inclusion.* Copyright © 2000, Corwin Press, Inc.

Sample of Student Services Director Responsibilities/Time Commitments

Management	Reactionary Leadership	Proactive Stewardship
Special education • Evaluation/placement decisions • Budget maintenance • Teaching and support staff caseloads • Adhering to state regulations • Extended school year	**Special education** • IDEA complaints • Problematic IEPs • Ineffective staff: evaluations/ observations • Mediation • Troubleshooting student needs • Discipline issues • Writing necessary policies and procedures • Budget support for unaccounted/ unexpected needs • Responding to teacher staff concerns • Interviews	**Special education** • Reauthorization (merging services and procedures) • Move from programs to services • Technical assistance with staff • Staffing • Developing and writing discretionary grants • Challenging necessary state and regulatory functions with adequate data • New staff evaluations/ observations • Interviews • Provide and arrange for staff development in specific subject areas (e.g., nonaversive behavioral techniques, standards for all students, functional assessments)
Section 504 • Updating staff procedures	**Section 504** • Attending 504 meetings • Mediation of 504 issues	**Section 504** • Merge procedures and guidelines with IDEA
Social work services • Responding to issues and concerns • Monthly meetings • Budgetary needs	**Social work services** • Family issues • County issues • Building-specific dilemmas	**Social work services** • Circle of influence/evolving roles • Evaluation/observation
Psychology services • Responding to issues and concerns • Monthly meetings • Budgetary needs	**Psychology services** • Eligibility guidelines • Student-specific issues • Evaluation/observation	**Psychology services** • Circles of influence/evolving roles • Evaluation/observation • Administrative site support
School guidance • Responding to issues and concerns • Monthly meetings • Budgetary needs	**School guidance** • New student needs • Records	**School guidance** • Circle of Influence/evolving roles • Evaluation/observation • Administrative site support • Evolving curriculum around student wellness

Colleen A. Capper, Elise Frattura, Maureen W. Keyes, *Meeting the Needs of Students of ALL Abilities: How Leaders Go Beyond Inclusion.* Copyright © 2000, Corwin Press, Inc.

HANDOUT 6.5. Administrative Responsibilities/Time Commitments

Management	Reactionary Leadership	Proactive Stewardship

Colleen A. Capper, Elise Frattura, Maureen W. Keyes, *Meeting the Needs of Students of ALL Abilities: How Leaders Go Beyond Inclusion.* Copyright © 2000, Corwin Press, Inc.

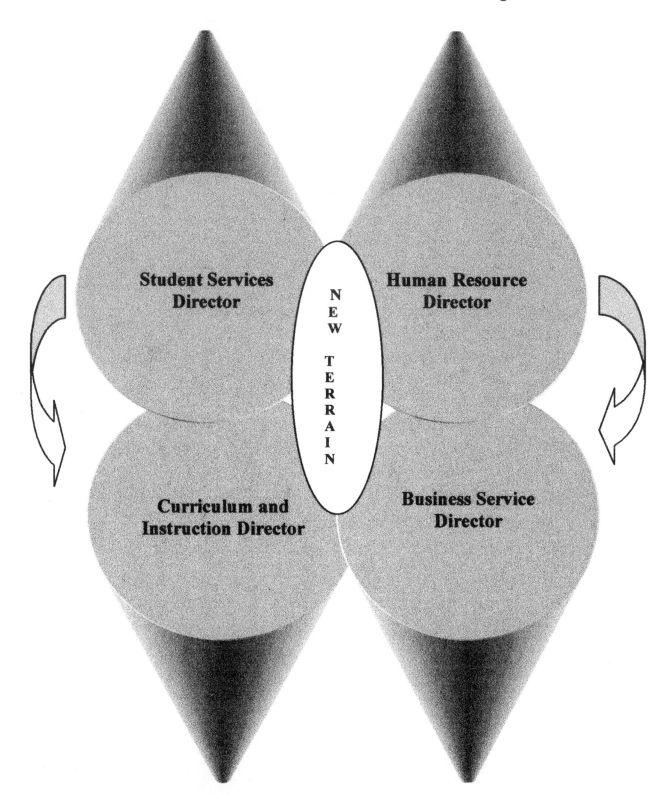

Colleen A. Capper, Elise Frattura, Maureen W. Keyes, *Meeting the Needs of Students of ALL Abilities: How Leaders Go Beyond Inclusion.* Copyright © 2000, Corwin Press, Inc.

HANDOUT 6.7. Teaching and Learning Facilitator

Student Services Director	Curriculum and Instruction Director	Teaching and Learning Facilitator K-5 or 6-12
• Policy about discrimination needs • Grant writing • Guidance and counseling • Student assistance and AODA programs • School-age parents (SAP) • Tuition requests • School social work services • School psychologist services • Screening for special education and early entrance • At-risk programs • Health and nursing services • Student records • ESL services • Gifted and talented services • Extended school year services • Exceptional educational programs • OT and PT • Special transportation	• C & I Committee • Library programming • All K-12 curriculum areas • Media services • Summer school • Staff development • Textbook selection • Title I • Student trips • Program evaluation • Standards and assessment	• **Curriculum for Each Learner** Facilitate growth of a differentiated curriculum devoted to teaching and supporting a range of learners • **Media and Technology Supports for Each Learner** Facilitate technology and other media that can be used across all students (e.g., for students with English as a second language, for students with vision and hearing loss, for students with processing difficulties, auditory learners, visual learners) • **Policy Development in Support of Each Learner** Nondiscrimination language in support of all learners • **Support Services for Each Learner** Development, implementation, and evaluation of support services for all students (e.g., guidance, social work, curriculum and/or behavioral facilitators) • **Content, Proficiency, and Performance Standards for Each Learner** Development, implementation, and evaluation of standards and benchmarks (from highly theoretical to extremely functional) in support of all learners • **Standardized and Individualized Educational Evaluation Procedures for Each Learner** Development, implementation, and evaluation of normative and individualized assessment for all students • **Staff Development in Support of Each Learner** Facilitation of in service, technical assistance, and other informative sessions in support of all students • **Financial Support for the Education of Each Learner** Assist in the merger of resources to meet the needs of each learner

Colleen A. Capper, Elise Frattura, Maureen W. Keyes, *Meeting the Needs of Students of ALL Abilities: How Leaders Go Beyond Inclusion.* Copyright © 2000, Corwin Press, Inc.

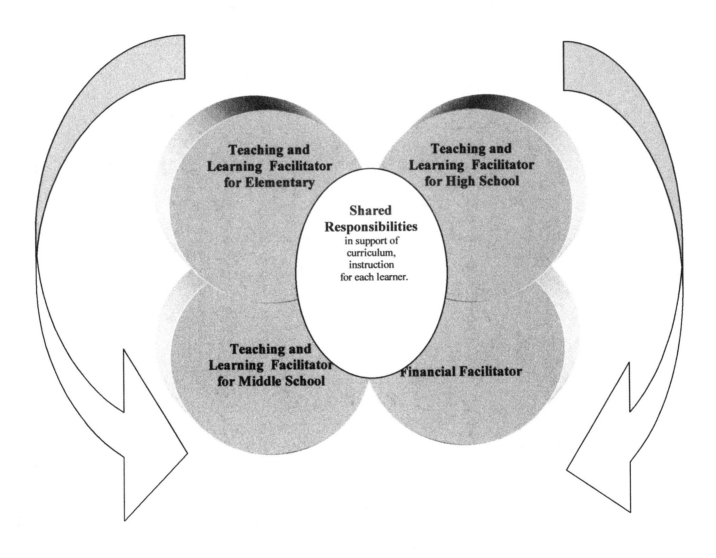

HANDOUT 6.8. Teaching and Learning Facilitator

Teaching and Learning Facilitator for Elementary

Teaching and Learning Facilitator for High School

Shared Responsibilities in support of curriculum, instruction for each learner.

Teaching and Learning Facilitator for Middle School

Financial Facilitator

Self-Evaluation:
Leading Beyond Inclusion

Directions: Complete the following Likert-type scale by rating the level of success, as well as delineating strengths/limitations, the next steps that should be taken, and what the timeline might look like.

5 = How we do business; 4 = Increased comfort level; 3 = Beginning implementation;
2 = Emerging through conversation; 1 = Yet to acknowledge as a need

Focus Area Chapter 6: The Central Office Must Walk the Talk	Likert-type Scale	Strengths/ Limitations	Next Steps	Timeline
Major area of emphasis:				
1. Central office administrators have asked the necessary questions to begin the analysis process (inquiry analysis).	5 4 3 2 1			
2. Central office administrators have completed a role analysis.	5 4 3 2 1			
3. Central office administrators have determined possible overlap in their roles and areas where they might collaborate.	5 4 3 2 1			
4. Central office administrators have moved out of their typical roles and have begun to collaborate in specific areas.	5 4 3 2 1			
5. Central office has merged some of the more apparent roles, such as curriculum and instruction and student services.	5 4 3 2 1			
6. Central office has evolved to a service delivery model in support of each student.	5 4 3 2 1			

Comments:

Colleen A. Capper, Elise Frattura, Maureen W. Keyes, *Meeting the Needs of Students of ALL Abilities: How Leaders Go Beyond Inclusion.* Copyright © 2000, Corwin Press, Inc.

Part II

Establish a Broad Range of Standards

As described in Part I, educators must first shift from programs to services to meet the needs of students of all abilities. Second, educators must establish a broad range of standards for student success. Many states have adopted standards and require that all students must pass high-stake state assessments to move to the next grade level or to graduate from high school. Districts can no longer merely exempt students from meeting requirements or from participating in assessments. If a student does not pass the state assessment, the district must prove the student can meet the standards and benchmarks through an alternative assessment procedure. Unlike this narrow interpretation of standards, however, that concentrates solely on academic areas, in this part of the book we argue that educators must first establish standards for emotional and physical safety (Chapter 7). Without such standards, many students will not experience the safety they need to do their best learning. In Chapter 8, we show educators six stages to developing curriculum standards to meet individual student needs. We include specific examples of how creative use of the standards can proactively inform teaching and assessment (Chapters 9 and 10). Along with academic standards, school leaders must hold students accountable for their behavior, and in Chapter 11 we identify standards for student behavior that move beyond suspension and expulsion.

Chapter 7

Standards for Physical and Emotional Safety

Prerequisites for Student Success[1]

The violence in public schools in recent years shows the crucial need for schools to work harder to ensure the physical and emotional safety of students. Often, violent acts arise from situations in which peers have abused students in the school—emotionally or verbally—over years. The research is clear that within-school harassment not addressed leads to more severe forms of abuse and violence in schools. Sadly, often adults in schools hesitate to intervene when peers or other adults in the school harass students. For example, 97% of students in public high schools report regularly hearing homophobic remarks from their peers, and 53% of students report hearing homophobic comments by school staff (Governor's Commission on Gay and Lesbian Youth, 1993). The Safe Schools Coalition in Washington reports in its 1998 annual survey that in 4 years its study team had

> gathered information about 91 incidents [of harassment] in 59 public schools and one private school. Incidents have included gang rapes (8 cases), physical assaults (19 incidents), physical harassment (14 reports), and verbal and other harassment (34 cases). Students have been kicked, punched, and attacked with weapons. They have sustained broken bones, contusions, and cuts. One person was vomited upon. Another was urinated upon. Forty-one incidents were serious enough to warrant criminal allegations. *Adults witnessed more than a fourth of the instances, yet they were unrespon-*

AUTHORS' NOTE: We acknowledge the many helpful ideas of Timothy Lee, former middle school principal and currently director of Wingra School; and Steve Hartley, principal of Shabazz High School, Madison, Wisconsin.

sive in half of those cases [italics added]. Six of those targeted changed schools, nine dropped out of school, eight attempted suicide and one committed suicide. (p. 2)

Besides a culture of verbal and emotional abuse that often exists in schools, many students arrive at school with unexpressed feelings because of tension in the home or overexposure to television, computer, or video game violence. These students may feel intense and agitated and thus more easily triggered by perhaps routine but frustrating situations at school. If these students lack the skills to deal with their emotions or to work out conflict in healthy ways, these students tend to move to "fighting level."

Not only do students have a *right* to feel safe at school, but for learning to occur, students *need* to feel safe. Recent research on the brain and learning suggests that when a person feels afraid, the brain shuts down, making learning very difficult. The U.S. Supreme Court has also ruled that school administrators now have a legal responsibility to protect students from harassment. Teachers and administrators can be held legally liable for failing to stop harassment in the school (Reese, 1997).

Schools that have experienced the most success in creating a safe learning community and in thwarting harassment share several interconnected strategies. From these proactive strategies in these schools, we identify five standards for emotional and physical safety: (a) make physical and emotional safety central to all aspects of the school, (b) establish a culture of inclusivity and visibility, (c) take harassment seriously: zero tolerance, (d) cocreate antiharassment policy and strategies, and (e) integrate antiharassment into the curriculum (see Handout 7.1).

Standard 1: Make Physical and Emotional Safety Central to All Aspects of the School

Like the other strategies outlined in this book, creating and nurturing safe schools by dealing with harassment and by taking a proactive stance against it is not another "add-on" initiative in schools that are successful with these efforts. Educators in these schools believe that all students and staff deserve to learn and work in an emotionally and physically safe environment. In fact, learning and successful work cannot occur in schools that are unsafe. Successful schools centrally integrate these ideas into their mission statement (see Resource D for one example). Simply printing the antiharassment policy in the student handbook and discussing it briefly on the first day of school is not enough.

A culture of emotional and physical safety is not served or supported when students or staff believe that adults in the school are held to a different standard than students. Many educators have shared with us incidences of adults not responding to student-to- student harassment, adults making disparaging remarks in the classroom about students, and adults making disparaging remarks about individuals or groups of individuals to other adults. Statistics that cite the lack of adult response to student harassment and the degree of harassing comments made by adults about students suggest that the school administrator must model and insist that safe school policies and practices apply to all adults and students.

Teachers have also cited incidences of teacher-to-teacher harassment that have not been addressed. For example, one teacher reported how he was harassed daily in the teachers' lounge by older, female teachers about his looks that included remarks about his body. Without a clear antiharassment policy at his school, he felt powerless and unable to confront these teachers, especially as a new, untenured teacher in the school. Other teachers cite teachers' lounge talk that includes a barrage of sexual jokes or jokes that demean individuals or groups of people, particularly homosexuals. Administrators must make it clear that they will not tolerate sexual innuendo and other offensive talk on school grounds, including teachers' lounges. We need to include the adults in the school in all the standards we describe here. We must hold students and adults to the same safe school standards.

Standard 2: Establish a Culture of Inclusivity and Visibility

Schools that are emotionally and physically safe for students are grounded in a culture of inclusivity. Too often, school administrators spend more time on sanctions and consequences of harassment than on building the prerequisites to preventing harassment from occurring in the first place. For example, large schools and an atmosphere of competition contribute to student alienation and disengagement that sows the seeds for students hurting each other. Building smaller schools, dividing large schools into families or smaller house units (McPartland, Jordan, Legters, & Balfanz, 1997), and developing curriculum and instruction based on cooperation and collaboration (Johnson, Johnson, Hodne, & Stevahn, 1997) are all prerequisites to student emotional and social safety.

Emotional and physical safety also begins with visibility. Students, staff, and parents need to be able to walk into a school and see themselves represented in the pictures, posters, artwork, and other decor within the school halls, common areas, administrative offices, and classrooms. They need to be able to see themselves and positive representations of themselves in the curriculum, in the library and other media materials, and in the texts and materials used in the classroom.

After responding to the demographic questions in Chapter 3 (see Resource B), assess your school/district culture. To what extent does your school/district culture visually represent the demographics of your school/district? One school we visited displayed Celebrate Diversity in big letters in the front entrance to the school. The hall walls featured many excellent pictures, poetry, and other artwork associated with African Americans. Hispanic students, Hmong students, students with disabilities, Asian students, gay/lesbian students, and students from gay/lesbian families, however, also attended this school. No cultural representations were on display for these students. Thus schools need to show their awareness and appreciation of all the students visibly in the school culture.

Standard 3: Take Harassment Seriously: Zero Tolerance

The key component of an antiharassment policy is zero tolerance; that is, students and staff need to know from the first day of school that harassment in any form will not be tolerated in the school and that everyone in the school will consistently respond to harassment as outlined in the school's antiharassment policy.

Adults may fail to take action when students hurl insults at one another. Administrators have told us, "That's just how it is in middle school." "John is complaining about being teased, but we cannot prove it, so what can I do?" and "That's a PC [politically correct] term. We can't say anything around here!" (see Handout 7.2 for a list of harassment myths and "dangerous words" to consider when working with students or adults who hurt one another). Some staff may feel burdened by being required to call students on every incident. We cannot simply ignore students who hurt one another in schools. Staff must make the time and take these complaints seriously to prevent escalation of the situation and to prevent students who are harassed from harboring anger and resentment over time.

Besides being conscious of how they respond to a student or staff member who reports being hurt in some way, school leaders must also be careful where they focus their efforts and not intentionally punish the person who has been hurt or abused. For example, one middle school principal we worked with was concerned how the males in classrooms often intimidated females at her school. These young women were afraid to contribute to class discussions or to offer responses to teacher questions. This principal's initial strategy was to work with these female students to help them be more assertive. Although this strategy could be helpful, these females could infer from this strategy that the intimidating classroom climate was somehow their fault and that if they changed their behavior, the atmosphere would be different. After time to think, the principal agreed that she needed to work also with the teaching staff on ways to change the classroom climate to be most conducive to all students participating. She worked with the teachers to learn teaching strategies to counterbalance the gender inequities that often silence females in classrooms (see Sadker & Sadker, 1995).

Standard 4: Cocreate Antiharassment Policy and Strategies

Schools that have experienced the most success with nurturing the emotional well-being of students actively involve students and staff in creating policies and strategies that support students and that thwart school abuse. Students from kindergarten through 12th grade can actively participate in the process. Administrators and teachers need to ensure that they do not invite just the "good" students to participate in this work. Students who struggle are often the most astute observers of school safety because many have experienced firsthand what it feels like not to belong. We should also invite parents, including parents who are not as visible in the school as other parents.

One of the first tasks of the committee's work is defining harassment. Cherokee Middle School in Madison, Wisconsin, defined *harassment* this way: "Any mean look, word, or act that hurts a person's body, belongings, or feelings." Becoming clear about harassment is an ongoing process. Know that it is the effect of a person's behavior, and not the intent, that is important; that is, a person may not intend to offend another, but he or she does, and it angers the other person. The offender then needs to take responsibility for his or her actions.

Standard 5: Integrate Antiharassment Into the Curriculum

Students profit most from antiharassment efforts when they can learn why particular behaviors may cause distress in others. Educators must remember: education first, then consequences. Staff and students need to capitalize on teachable moments when dealing with harassment. Students and staff need to know not only the definition of harassment but also why such behavior is offensive and the history of offensive remarks, and students need to recognize the negative effects of their behavior.

Besides taking advantage of informal, teachable moments when harassment occurs, we need to teach antiharassment specifically and to engage students in activities that further their learning. One way to integrate antiharassment efforts into the curriculum is to teach conflict management to all students. Frequently, only students identified as "good students" are selected to participate in learning conflict resolution. This selection process serves only to perpetuate stereotypes and hierarchy in the classroom. All students should have the opportunity to learn these skills. Some schools specifically select students who have struggled with their own behavior because it places these students in positions of responsibility that serves to moderate their behavior.

A second way to integrate antiharassment into the curriculum and the culture of the school is to require a course or two in learning about differences. For example, Shabazz High School in Madison, Wisconsin, requires all incoming students to enroll in Shabazz I and Shabazz II. These two courses, cotaught by an instructor and returning students, introduce incoming students to the culture and expectations of the school. The courses also include curriculum and instruction related to antiracism, understanding religious differences, gender equity, and other areas of difference (see Resource D for an example of case studies used in these courses to teach students about the antiharassment policy).

Conducting antiharassment workshops that students have designed and presented is a third way to integrate these efforts into the curriculum. For example, at Cherokee Middle School, students conduct educational training for the entire school that includes role plays in each homeroom. Students put the issue in their own words. As part of the workshop, students are asked to write responses to the open sentence "I feel safe when . . ." Student responses are then posted throughout the school. When working with students to design class lessons or workshops, educators should ensure that a variety of students participate. These experiences should reflect and model the content of the workshop about respecting differences (see Resource D for excerpts from a workshop).

We can also integrate antiharassment within classroom teaching. For example, Lenore Gordon (1983) describes a lesson on name calling that she has used with students at all grade levels. In summary, the lesson includes the following components:

1. Ask students to brainstorm names they have been called or they have heard others called in their classroom or school.

2. List all suggestions on the chalkboard.

3. Categorize the names (e.g., racial, ethnic, sexual, religious, body size, intellectual ability).

4. Discuss that all name calling involves prejudice and is equally bad.

5. Make it clear that you will not tolerate any form of name calling.

6. Explain why and discuss consequences for failure to adhere to the rule.

7. Immediately respond to any transgressions.

Handout 7.3 lists the results of the first step of this lesson with second graders. The list shows the extent to which children experience name calling and other hurtful behavior at school even at young ages. If a teacher works in a school or district that is failing to address harassment issues, along with promoting antiharassment efforts in his or her school, implementing activities such as this lesson plan can make a marked difference in the classroom.

With education and awareness about harassment, educators can expect an upswing in incidences. At one school, students began using "harassment" frivolously. We can lessen the likelihood that this will happen if we have integrated antiharassment work throughout the year and not confined it to the beginning of the year.

Examples of an Antiharassment Policy in Practice

Resource D includes a copy of the Shabazz High School antiharassment policy. Here, we share a few examples of this policy in practice.

Antiharassment policies need to include details on responding to harassment. The Shabazz policy gives a person who feels harassed three options: (a) respectfully confront the sender, (b) contact a teacher or other staff member, or (c) contact an administrator. Students can learn how to confront someone respectfully who they believe is harassing them. Along with this learning, they can learn to assess the power dynamics of the situation and determine whether a safer response might be to inform a teacher or administrator. For example, a student may be afraid of saying "Stop it!" to another student who is physically bigger than him or her and threatens a beating. Or a student may feel intimidated to voice his or her opposition to the behavior of a teacher the student believes is harassing.

"Giving Notice"

At Shabazz High School, when a student reports to an adult that someone is harassing him or her, the adult discusses the incident with the student and inquires whether the student asked the person to stop this behavior. The adult takes brief notes at this meeting. Then the adult gives the alleged perpetrator notice. This means the adult enters into a dialogue with the student. Talking with the accused student should be considered educational. For example, the adult can say, "I have been told of complaints about you. I don't have proof, but I am getting these complaints. I will be letting the staff know. We'll begin to go down this path." Be specific on what the complaint is and what the consequences are. "I am giving notice to you. This is what the student/staff is saying. What's going on?" "What you have said is being interpreted this way." If the harassment is persistent or significant, the adult makes a follow-up call to the alleged perpetrator's parent. The principal is informed right away about the complaint.

Administrators and other educators should keep an ongoing incident file. They should take notes while they are talking with the students and keep a building team log. This record keeping helps the educators track students and agreements they have worked out with students, aiding accountability.

In sum, how does your school or district measure up, based on our five standards for physical and emotional safety? Students count on adults to create emotionally and physically safe spaces in which they learn and grow. We have to model and practice preventive strategies for giving students this basic need. When students feel safe, educators can work toward academic standards.

Educators must remember, however, that when establishing academic standards for all students, many students may reach these standards without any challenge. Standards that treat all students the same are as detrimental for these students as they are for students who may never reach the standards. We show educators how to individualize curriculum standards for each student in Chapter 8.

Note

1. We also believe that intellectual safety is of equal importance in the school, but addressing this topic thoroughly is beyond the scope of this chapter.

HANDOUT 7.1. Standards for Physical and Emotional Safety

Standard 1:   Make physical and emotional safety central to all aspects of the school.

Standard 2:   Establish a culture of inclusivity and visibility.

Standard 3:   Take harassment seriously: zero tolerance.

Standard 4:   Cocreate antiharassment policy and strategies.

Standard 5:   Integrate antiharassment into the curriculum.

Colleen A. Capper, Elise Frattura, Maureen W. Keyes, *Meeting the Needs of Students of ALL Abilities: How Leaders Go Beyond Inclusion*. Copyright © 2000, Corwin Press, Inc.

HANDOUT 7.2. Harassment Myths and Dangerous Words

When responding to a complaint, be careful that these words do not come out of your mouth.

- It's just teasing—no big deal.
- If we had to discipline every student who used bad language, we'd never get anything else done.
- This kind of behavior is all part of growing up.
- It's a matter of hormones; we can't control that.
- It's just a joke. Lighten up.
- That's how they do things where he comes from.
- Just ignore it.
- You need to learn to handle these things.
- It's your fault for dressing so provocatively (differently, etc.).
- Oh, well. Boys will be boys.
- It's just a prank that got out of hand.
- We've never had a complaint, so we don't have a problem.
- No one's filed a charge, so our hands are tied.
- You must have wanted it; otherwise, you would have told him no.
- Why can't you learn to accept a compliment?
- She puts her arms around everyone.
- I know he (or she) didn't mean anything like that.
- The people in our school would never do . . .

SOURCE: This material is adapted by permission of the *Educator's Guide to Controlling Sexual Harassment*, Thompson Publishing Group, 1725 K Street N.W., Washington D.C. (tel: 1-800-677-3789). Thompson Publishing Group retains its copyright to this material.

HANDOUT 7.3.

List of Names a Class of Second-Grade Students Had Been Called
or Had Heard Others Called in Their School

S-WORD

DUCK

JERK

LITTLE OLD MAN

FRAIDY CAT

BUCK TOOTH

LITTLE DORK

CHICKEN

YUK

HOMELESS

STUPID

IDIOT

PUNK

NEGRO

BLACK NIGGER

BUTTHEAD

RETARD

STUPID HEAD

COW

SLOW POKE

A-WORD

DICK HEAD

LOSER

FAT HEAD

GREEDY

FAT

LITTLE KID

PUSSY

4-EYES

DUMB

BOY

FAGGOT

SKINNY

B-WORD

STINK BOMB

BIG HEAD

PIG

RETARDED

FATSO

STINK

BONY

LITTLE BOY

RAT

PUMPKIN HEAD

"YOU'LL BE LIVING OUT IN THE STREETS, AND I'LL BE LAUGHING"

BIG EYES

FAT GORILLA

FREAK

WIMP

SLUG

NIGGER

NOTE: We appreciate the work of Kate Lyman, teacher at Hawthorne Elementary School, Madison, Wisconsin, for sharing the results of her lesson on name calling with us.

Self-Evaluation:
Leading Beyond Inclusion

Directions: Complete the following Likert-type scale by rating the level of success, as well as delineating strengths/limitations, the next steps that should be taken, and what the timeline might look like.

5 = How we do business; 4 = Increased comfort level; 3 = Beginning implementation;
2 = Emerging through conversation; 1 = Yet to acknowledge as a need

Focus Area *Chapter 7: Standards for Physical and Emotional Safety: Prerequisites for Student Success*	Likert-type Scale	Strengths/ Limitations	Next Steps	Timeline
Major area of emphasis:				
1. Physical and emotional safety is central to all aspects of the school.	5 4 3 2 1			
2. Our mission statement reflects our commitment to physical and emotional safety.	5 4 3 2 1			
3. Adults are held to the same standards as students for remarks and behavior.	5 4 3 2 1			
4. We have a culture of inclusivity and visibility for all people in the halls, classrooms, and common areas.	5 4 3 2 1			
5. We spend more time on preventing harassment than on sanctions.	5 4 3 2 1			
6. Our curriculum, library, media, texts, and other materials reflect the range of diversity.	5 4 3 2 1			
7. We take harassment seriously and do not ignore offensive student remarks.	5 4 3 2 1			
8. We do not "blame the victim" when dealing with harassment.	5 4 3 2 1			

		5 4 3 2 1	
9.	We are familiar with harassment myths and work to not act on these myths.	5 4 3 2 1	
10.	We cocreate antiharassment policy with students, parents, and staff.	5 4 3 2 1	
11.	All students have an opportunity to participate in policy development, including students who struggle in school.	5 4 3 2 1	
12.	We have a clear definition of harassment.	5 4 3 2 1	
13.	We take a zero tolerance position on harassment.	5 4 3 2 1	
14.	We integrate antiharassment into the curriculum.	5 4 3 2 1	
15.	We take action based on education first, then consequences.	5 4 3 2 1	
16.	All students have an opportunity to teach and facilitate related topics with other students.	5 4 3 2 1	
17.	All students are skilled in conflict resolution and mediation.	5 4 3 2 1	
18.	We require courses or workshops on learning about differences and the cultures of the school.	5 4 3 2 1	
19.	Our training is ongoing throughout the year.	5 4 3 2 1	
20.	Antiharassment is integrated into classroom teaching.	5 4 3 2 1	

Comments:

Colleen A. Capper, Elise Frattura, Maureen W. Keyes, *Meeting the Needs of Students of ALL Abilities: How Leaders Go Beyond Inclusion.* Copyright © 2000, Corwin Press, Inc.

Chapter 8

Developing Curriculum Standards

Educators are implementing academic standards and accountability through "smart" goals, data-driven student learning, and assessments for all students. If we continue to blaze ahead blindly, accountability and high expectations for all students will do more damage than good for the students they were intended to protect and educate. If the goal of educators is to challenge all students with high academic standards and to teach and measure performance in the same way for all students, then educators will continue to fail the same 10% to 20% of the nation's children who currently are failing. According to Reigeluth (1997), standards and assessments "can be used as tools for standardization—to help make all students alike. Or they can be used as tools for customization—to help meet individual students' needs" (p. 203). In this chapter, we agree with the latter opinion—the individualization of standards.

Across the nation, school districts have launched into developing standards of success for all students without answering two major questions: (a) What if a student cannot meet the standards? and (b) What if a student meets the standards but the teaching and assessment for the standards do not in any way challenge the student? We typically ignore the students whose abilities far exceed the standards. For the other students, often the response is "If we set high standards for all students, all students will rise to the occasion." Students will not just rise to the occasion without appropriate instruction and an individualized standard for learning. Often, educators replace the standards for students who struggle with goals from the students' individualized educational plan (IEP for students labeled with a disability or receiving services through Section 504). Rather than designing individually appropriate standards, these educators decide to opt these students out of the standards and assessments. If we do not adopt individualized educational standards for those students who were the reason such "high-powered standards" were initiated, then students will continue to fail. Here, we suggest some do's and don'ts when creating curricular standards to meet the needs of students of all abilities, followed by six steps for designing individualized curriculum standards.

Do's and Don'ts When Creating Curriculum Standards

Do not use grade retention and withholding of diplomas as the primary response to students who do not meet the standards. We agree with Darling-Hammond and Falk (1997), who suggest, "We need to use standards and authentic assessments as indicators of progress for improved teaching, not as gateways to grade transition" (p. 198). The research is clear about the problems with retention, including that retention results in

- Poorer self-concepts
- More problems with social adjustments
- Students feeling more negative toward school
- An increased risk of dropping out by 40% to 50%

Moreover, retention is third on the list of a child's greatest fears—behind blindness and death of a parent (Darling-Hammond & Falk, 1997). These researchers further explain that "retention ignores the question of whether the child was taught appropriately the first time, whether new strategies might be needed to support learning, whether the educational environment itself, rather than the child, is lacking" (p. 192). Further, retaining a student for 1 year raises the cost of educating that student by 8%.

Do discuss what will happen to students who fail to meet the standards. Most of a school's or district's work should address the question, What do we do with students who may not meet the standard? A primary goal of the standards movement is to bring up to standard those students who are struggling. We should spend as much time on developing creative responses for students who may not meet the standards as we do on setting standards and creating assessments.

Do not assume that the standards have nothing to do with student services staff. Do include special services staff on standards committees in the district and in staff development related to the standards. All special education and student services staff should be integrally involved in district/school standards work. These staff members, perhaps more than any other, have expertise in setting standards (long-term goals), benchmarks (short-term objectives), and creative teaching and assessment practices. These educators also may be most familiar with the scope and sequence of the curriculum and working with students to achieve these goals and objectives.

Do not assume that the primary problem in student achievement is student motivation and that students are best motivated by fear. Do assume that teachers and educators bear equal responsibility to standards. Do hold teachers as accountable as students. Legislation based on student results versus teacher initiatives seems to be more accepted and easier to take because the responsibility falls on the learner rather than on the instructor. Hilliard (1998) agrees:

> To establish standards of output without having standards of input is a travesty. To hold children responsible for outcomes without giving them the same level of sophisticated attention to guaranteeing the standards of exposure is an abandonment of responsibility of adults for the education and socialization of children. (p. 4)

We need to develop standards of service delivery for teachers and administrators.

Do encourage all educators to take responsibility for the quality of educational experience students receive. Do not shift accountability to teachers without providing teachers the resources and support they need to be successful. As we described in Chapter 5, principals and other administrators must give teachers all the support and resources they need to be able to succeed with a wide range of student needs, including general ongoing support, staff development, resources and materials, and time and scheduling support.

Do not totally ignore or get stuck on how to deal with the 1% of the student population who might need something different to prevent us from holding high expectations for all students. We need to consider all students in the development of standards, including students with significantly different intellectual and emotional needs. A person who can represent these students should be assigned to every standards committee/meeting. At the same time, we need to raise our expectations of all students, including students with labels. Standards can reduce stereotyping by teachers that some students (e.g., students from lower social classes, ESL students) are unable to achieve more. Standards can also lessen the enabling and overaccommodations that can sometimes happen with students labeled with disabilities.

Six Steps for Designing Individualized Curriculum Standards

Besides these basic do's and don'ts for developing curriculum standards, we have also identified six steps for educators to use in developing high academic standards that we individualize for each student. We describe these steps more fully next (see also Handout 8.1).

Step 1: Determine the Attainment Level/Cluster at Which the Student Is Working

Currently, the standards are based on grade-level performance expectations. All educators know, however, that children do not learn and develop at the same rate. Therefore, it does not make sense to hold students to the artificial parameters of age-level standards when in all actuality we want them to be able to progress from their current achievement level to the next level. We should define standards in age-/grade-level clusters, and then teachers can freely move across the standards on the basis of individual need. For example, Erin, age 9, may be extremely literate in social studies and science, well beyond her fourth-grade peers, but require additional time in math, where she functions closer to the second-grade level. Erin's standards, curriculum, and assessment instrument may represent two or three different age/grade levels for the range of content standards (see Handout 8.2).

Step 2: Determine the Desired Standard/Long-Range Goal

A statement of desired outcome is necessary as a long-term goal for each standard area. The general timeline for a goal is 1 year. For example, in math, Erin can show that she can construct or select and use a variety of appropriate strategies to solve problems from real-world situations. The long-term intended outcome (concept or principle) or desired behavior may be broader in nature than if one were to begin with a skill or skill cluster.

Step 3: Determine the Related Benchmarks/ Objectives for Each Standard/Goal

Related benchmarks or short-term objectives are subsets of the long-range goal. The student must reach these intermediate objectives on the way to achieving the goal. For Erin to meet the math standard, she must be able to demonstrate that she knows the associated benchmarks to that goal. Here, her math benchmarks include "Write a number sentence to solve problems and solve problems using computer software, calculators, or math manipulatives."

Step 4: Determine the Methods of Instruction for Each Benchmark/Objective

Instructional options must be the most important area of content standards, and we should design them to meet the learning styles and interests of students. Some features associated with effective curriculum and instruction for some students may be at odds with the curriculum typically embraced by standards-based reform. Therefore, instruction must allow a heterogeneous group of students to achieve to their individual potential (Tomlinson, 1999; see Chapter 9 for information about standards-based instruction).

Step 5: Determine How to Measure/ Assess the Instruction

We must measure what we teach by a range of assessments: standardized, performance-based, functional, or individualized assessments (see Chapter 10 for details). Such a range will allow students to demonstrate understanding from paper-and-pencil tests to application. In this way, we will not dually assess students on their ability to "test perform" and on their ability to have content knowledge. Assessment must be meaningful and applicable to the specific learner and her or his individualized benchmarks.

Step 6: Determine the Performance Level That Defines Success for Each Student

We must define success for each student along a continuum of success factors based on a criterion-reference-based process. That is, we must reinforce a student for progress toward her or his goals versus a normative reference that marks success or failure against a peer group. Such learner-based accountability procedures allow students to build on positive experiences and challenge themselves, instead of overcoming academic failures when compared with peers.

Handout 8.3 contains the standards, curriculum, and assessment template we can use to develop options to show success for all students. This instrument assumes that a range of curriculum strategies and assessments is available to all students and that accountability is not limited to a single assessment or teaching strategy. Through such a process, we remove grade levels from the standards and then apply a variety of levels of attainment (Reigeluth, 1997). With this process, we can use the standards and benchmarks as guides for instruction and calibrate assessments to individual student learning needs.

We can use the standards, curriculum, and assessment template in place of the grade-level report card and individualized instructional plans. The blank form in Handout 8.3 can be used to add standards in areas not currently covered by state or district standards. We can take such standards from the arts, physical education, community service projects, and specific areas for students currently using an individualized educational plan (IEP for Section 504 or students meeting eligibility for special education services).

The instrument can be kept in a database under each student's identification number. In this way, a range of individuals (e.g., current teachers, parent or legal guardian, counselors, building principal) can access the database and add information (fire walls can be built to prevent tampering with the data). Teachers can add information regularly (e.g., daily, weekly, monthly, grading period). Within the student's computerized data folder, we can establish individual files for each assessment: a performance-based assessment file, a standardized assessment file, a functional assessment file, and an individualized assessment file (see Chapter 10 for explanation). Further, we can establish files for extracurricular activities and information for graduation requirements. In so doing, each student can have a standards and curriculum assessment instrument that represents the targeted standards and other areas of need.

With this 6-stage process, we can hold students to individualized curriculum expectations that truly challenge them to achieve to their highest potential. We must also individualize assessments for students, and we explain how to do so in Chapter 9.

HANDOUT 8.1. Developing Standards: Six Steps to Meet Individual Student Needs

Step 1: Determine the attainment level/cluster at which the student is working.

Step 2: Determine the desired standard/long-range goal.

Step 3: Determine the related benchmarks/objectives for each standard/goal.

Step 4: Determine the methods of instruction for each benchmark/objective.

Step 5: Determine how to measure/assess the instruction.

Step 6: Determine the performance level that defines success for each student.

Age/Grade cluster	Curriculum standard (long-term objective)	Related benchmarks for stated standard	Primary methodology for instruction	Assessment options	Performance level
2-4 grade	**Reading** Read to acquire information	• Summarize key details of informational texts, connecting new information to prior knowledge. • Identify a topic of interest and seek information about it by investigating available text resources.	☐ Experiential ☐ Functional ☐ Small group ☐ Cooperative ☐ Tutorial ☐ Other	☐ Performance-based ☐ Functional ☐ District assessment with modifications ☐ State assessment with modifications ☐ Portfolio ☐ Observation ☐ Other	☐ Advanced ☐ Proficient ☐ Basic skills ☐ Developing skills ☐ Supplanting skills ☐ Other
2-4 grade	**Math** Construct or select and use a variety of appropriate strategies to solve problems from real-world situations.	• Solve problems using different strategies such as draw a picture, build a model, act out, or look for a pattern. • Write number sentences to solve problems. • Solve problems using computer software, calculators, and/or math manipulatives.	☐ Experiential ☐ Functional ☐ Small group ☐ Cooperative ☐ Tutorial ☐ Other	☐ Performance-based ☐ Functional ☐ District assessment with modifications ☐ State assessment with modifications ☐ Portfolio ☐ Observation ☐ Other	☐ Advanced ☐ Proficient ☐ Basic skills ☐ Developing skills ☐ Supplanting skills ☐ Other

Colleen A. Capper, Elise Frattura, Maureen W. Keyes, *Meeting the Needs of Students of ALL Abilities: How Leaders Go Beyond Inclusion.* Copyright © 2000, Corwin Press, Inc.

HANDOUT 8.3. Standards, Curriculum, and Assessment Template for All Students

Age/Grade cluster	Curriculum standard (long-term objective)	Related benchmarks for stated standard	Primary methodology for instruction	Assessment options	Performance level
			☐ Experiential ☐ Functional ☐ Small group ☐ Cooperative ☐ Tutorial ☐ Other	☐ Performance-based ☐ Functional ☐ District assessment with modifications ☐ State assessment with modifications ☐ Portfolio ☐ Observation ☐ Other	☐ Advanced ☐ Proficient ☐ Basic skills ☐ Developing skills ☐ Supplanting skills ☐ Other
			☐ Experiential ☐ Functional ☐ Small group ☐ Cooperative ☐ Tutorial ☐ Other	☐ Performance-based ☐ Functional ☐ District assessment with modifications ☐ State assessment with modifications ☐ Portfolio ☐ Observation ☐ Other	☐ Advanced ☐ Proficient ☐ Basic skills ☐ Developing skills ☐ Supplanting skills ☐ Other

Colleen A. Capper, Elise Frattura, Maureen W. Keyes, *Meeting the Needs of Students of ALL Abilities: How Leaders Go Beyond Inclusion.*
Copyright © 2000, Corwin Press, Inc.

Self-Evaluation:
Leading Beyond Inclusion

Directions: Complete the following Likert-type scale by rating the level of success, as well as delineating strengths/limitations, the next steps that should be taken, and what the timeline might look like.

5 = How we do business; 4 = Increased comfort level; 3 = Beginning implementation;
2 = Emerging through conversation; 1 = Yet to acknowledge as a need

Focus Area *Chapter 8: Developing Curriculum Standards*	Likert-type Scale	Strengths/ Limitations	Next Steps	Timeline
Major area of emphasis:				
1. We do not use grade retention and withholding of diplomas as the primary response to students who do not meet the standards.	5 4 3 2 1			
2. We consider the needs of each student in standards work.	5 4 3 2 1			
3. We spend as much time developing creative responses for students who may not meet the standards as we do on setting standards and creating assessments.	5 4 3 2 1			
4. Special services staff serve as participants on all aspects and committees associated with the standards.	5 4 3 2 1			
5. We hold teachers as accountable as students for standards.	5 4 3 2 1			
6. We provide teachers the resources and support they need to be successful.	5 4 3 2 1			

(Continued)

Self-Evaluation *(Continued)*

5 = How we do business;   4 = Increased comfort level;   3 = Beginning implementation;
2 = Emerging through conversation;   1 = Yet to acknowledge as a need

Focus Area *Chapter 8: Developing Curriculum Standards*	*Likert-type Scale*	Strengths/ Limitations	Next Steps	Timeline
7. The district has adopted curriculum standards for each student, not standards for different groups of students (students with English as a second language or students receiving special education).	5 4 3 2 1			
8. A common template is used for each student to track individual learner progress.	5 4 3 2 1			
9. Standards are used across grade levels to meet better the individual needs of each learner.	5 4 3 2 1			
10. Differentiated curriculum is used and documented to meet better the needs of the individual learner.	5 4 3 2 1			
11. A range of different assessment options is used so students can demonstrate what they know best in a comfortable way.	5 4 3 2 1			

Comments:

Colleen A. Capper, Elise Frattura, Maureen W. Keyes, *Meeting the Needs of Students of ALL Abilities: How Leaders Go Beyond Inclusion.*
Copyright © 2000, Corwin Press, Inc.

Chapter 9

Standards-Based Teaching That Ensures Success

As we explained in Chapter 1 and as we illustrated with Colleen's experiences with her son's schools, the most important ingredient for meeting the needs of all students is effective instruction that meets the needs of students of all abilities. We can create heterogeneous classes with the full range of student abilities, we can reduce the sizes of classes, and we can design multiage classes where we do not group students by grade but by a range of ages. If the instruction in any of these configurations does not meet the needs of students of all abilities, however, then students will not achieve their highest potential. Tomlinson (1999) agrees:

> We have often claimed that such heterogenous classes represent high expectations for struggling learners, but we then leave them to their own devices to figure out how to "catch up" with the expectations. Such an approach does not result in genuine growth for struggling learners. (p. 22)

Districts and schools should reallocate into classroom instruction the money saved from moving from programs to services, from serving all students in their neighborhood schools rather than transporting them to other schools, and from decreasing the number of students referred for formal evaluations. We need to take the resources that are currently allocated to divide and separate some students and instead provide the highest quality instruction for all students.

In our quest for developing standards, our primary focus should be on how we teach, not solely on the results of student performance on standardized assessments. Teaching and learning are processes for the teacher and the learner, and academic standards are our road map. Nevertheless, many different instructional roads can lead to the same high achievement destination. We depict standards-based teaching as grounded in a context of effective curriculum and instruction measured by a range of assessments (see Chapter 10) that meet the needs of all students. Here, we describe eight standards for teaching to ensure student success (see also Handout 9.1).

Standard 1: Reduce Student-to-Teacher Ratios

Research shows that smaller class sizes, particularly in the early grades, are advantageous to all students, especially students who struggle in school. Many school districts are reducing class sizes in kindergarten through third grade to 1 teacher for every 15 students. One way to reduce class size is to require all support staff to assist in teaching duties (Darling-Hammond & Falk, 1997, see chap. 4). According to Darling-Hammond and Falk (1997), in U.S. schools 40% to 50% of staff members are not classroom teachers. Congruent with our discussion in Chapters 1 and 2 about providing services to students instead of placing them in separate programs, educators should reassign nonteaching staff, pull-out teachers, and specialists into teaching teams to support all students. Teaching teams may assist and teach struggling teachers to provide individually challenging instruction to a range of students.

Standard 2: Make Early Literacy a Priority

For many students who are violent, students who exhibit challenging behaviors, students who require expensive alternative school placements in high school, and youths who are incarcerated, the common denominator is their struggle with reading. Research is clear about what works. We agree with reading experts that some children are not learning to read and write commensurate with their potential because educators are not teaching them the way they learn best (Snow, Burns, & Griffin, 1998).

Findings from 260 studies embracing all known possible factors in reading success and failure provide converging evidence that the core deficit in reading comprehension is phonological awareness, which leads to difficulties in rapid and accurate decoding. Schools that have strong reading instruction (including phonemic awareness) in kindergarten and first grade significantly reduce the number of students identified as having a learning disability or referred to Title I (Enfield, 1988).

Children with low reading scores tend to stay behind and not catch up. We cannot wait for children to fail before we teach them to read. Research shows that if we provide students who are behind in reading skills a reading intervention at first or second grade, 82% catch up with their peers. If educators wait until third grade to provide reading intervention, only 46% of students catch up. If we do not provide a structured reading program until fourth grade, only 10% to 15% of students will match the reading achievement of their same-grade peers. Longitudinal studies show that of the children who are reading disabled in third grade 74% remain disabled in ninth grade (Lyon, 1991).

In addition, no single reading program can address the needs of all students. At a minimum, all students in every school and district should have access to at least the five reading options we suggest in Handout 9.2. Many students benefit from the general reading instruction in the classroom that typically consists of whole language, or whole language combined with general phonics instruction integrated into the curriculum. Some students, however, may need more specific instruction in phonics, comprehension, or written expression.

Typically, we offer students who struggle with reading remedial reading instruction, summer school, or an assigned volunteer to work with them. Besides the fact that this "special help" often removes the student from his or her peers, unfortunately this instruction often mimics the instruction the student has already received, albeit at a slower pace or with more teacher attention. Some students, however, despite pace and attention, need a different kind of instruction. Some districts do offer a different kind of instruction but provide only one alternative. They offer no other options. We have been quite disappointed in the reluctance of some schools and districts to make a range of reading options available to all students, many insisting that the one approach they offer as an alternative to the typical curriculum (e.g., remedial reading, specific programs such as Reading Recovery) should work for all students. There are many reasons for this reluctance: (a) the amount of time and resources that some districts have invested in particular reading programs does not leave much money left for additional alternatives; (b) teachers able to use such programs are reluctant to learn new or additional strategies and are reluctant to give up their one-to-one time with students; and, closely related, (c) districts may face political implications and possible challenges by teacher unions if they were to add additional alternatives. As a result, some schools and districts are extremely reluctant to admit that their one approach does not work for all students or to offer alternatives.

To ensure that early literacy takes first priority in teaching standards for the success of each student, we make the following recommendations:

1. All teachers, especially K-5, need to be reading experts—that is, just as adept at whole language approaches as they are with phonetic approaches and vice versa. Most university teacher preparation programs, including programs specifically geared to reading specialists, do not provide education in reading alternatives in their programs. Districts need to provide the resources necessary for comprehensive and ongoing staff development in reading for all teachers in kindergarten through eighth grade and for all teachers who assist students with reading in high schools.

2. All school administrators need to be familiar with the various reading approaches and to ensure that the teachers they hire either possess these skills or are willing to learn them.

3. We should require phonemic awareness as part of a balanced kindergarten curriculum.

4. We should provide all kindergartners phonemic awareness screening at the end of the kindergarten year, and for those who show a deficit we should provide a structured reading program in first grade.

5. We should offer all students and parents a full range of reading options.

6. Do not wait for children to fail before addressing their reading needs.

Standard 3: Provide Early Intervention and Prevention Without Labeling

To illustrate our discussion, next we describe scenarios of three elementary school principals who advocate for including all students.

- Scenario I: This predominantly white, upper-middle-income K-2 school has identified 13% of its students for special education and has labeled another 12% of its students "at risk."

- Scenario II: The principal of another school laughs and says, "I have staff members who want to label kids early . . . as if there are LD kids in kindergarten or first grade!"

- Scenario III: The principal announces to the staff that as few students as possible should be labeled and that the staff should do everything possible in their curriculum and instruction to have success with all students without separating them from their peers.

Here is one way to interpret Scenario I: Because the school has identified students, the students will receive the services they need early in their elementary education, and this will prevent further difficulties later. Readers could assume that this scenario matches our standard for early intervention. It does not. Along with all the labels that will remain with these students for at least the remainder of their education, if not their entire lives, many of these students are placed in separate programs. We discussed the problems with this model in Chapter 1.

In Scenario II, we agree with this principal's philosophy of not wanting to label students. However, what if students need additional assistance in these early grades? This principal's attitude unfortunately coincides with federal law that requires students to be 2 years behind in at least one subject area to qualify for some special services. Thus many educators wait until a student is 2 years behind before the student receives help from a special program. We witnessed one educator encouraging her peers not to provide remedial instruction during the summer so that students would have a better chance of "qualifying" for services.

We are closest in agreement with Scenario III and advocate for early intervention and prevention without labels. What would this look like in practice? At the end of kindergarten, we would assess the phonemic awareness of all students via formal assessment and informal observation and information from the teacher and parents to decide whether the child might benefit from more structured instruction in literacy. We would couple this assessment with a comprehensive review of this child's strengths and gifts.

Students who are identified probably could benefit from the fourth option on our menu of reading options (see Handout 9.2)—whole language instruction combined with structured, sequential, direct instruction in phonics—without separating this student from his or her peers.

It is crucial that we remediate but at the same time not label and segregate. We show how to do this in the next standard.

Standard 4: Configure Class Grouping to Meet Student Needs Without Labeling

In addition to whole-class teaching, at some point in each day all students should have opportunities to work in small groups with the classroom teacher and to receive targeted skill or knowledge development for their unique needs. For example, for reading, the teacher can work with a small group of students on a sequential phonetic curriculum each day for 30 minutes while the rest of the class engages in their own reading activities or while a support specialist teaches another small group (see Chapter 4). This support person (who may previously have served as a teacher, for example in special education, with students considered "at risk," remedial reading, or "gifted and talented") could work with the classroom teacher to analyze individual learning needs and to determine individually appropriate standards, curriculum, and assessment practices in reading. The teacher then teaches some of the reading techniques he or she uses with these students (e.g., multisensory activities for learning to spell words phonetically and for learning specific grammar rules) with all the students in the class. In this way, students who need a little more direct instruction can serve as role models and peer instructors for the rest of the class.

The teacher also mixes students into mixed-ability groups for reading instruction in addition to the 30-minute skill-focused instructional time. Throughout the day, students interchange among groups along with independent work. To limit stereotyping and labeling, the teacher never groups students by the same ability in the same group throughout the day.

When configuring the class in this way, we accomplish several objectives:

- All students receive, at some point in their day, small-group instruction based on their individual needs.

- Student needs are identified, not ignored, and help is provided without labels.

- Students do not have to fail before receiving the support they need.

- All students' needs are addressed without students needing to be separated from their peers.

- The teacher benefits from the joy of seeing all students progress with his or her guidance. The teacher need not doubt his or her skills with students of varying abilities or delegate students to the "experts."

Now that the teacher has configured the class to ensure student success, what curriculum strategies support all students?

Standard 5: Ensure That All Students Have Access to Quality Teaching

According to Darling-Hammond and Falk (1997, p. 193), research on schools that meet high standards with diverse populations employ the following successful teaching strategies (see Handout 9.3):

- Offer students challenging, interesting activities and rich materials for learning that foster thinking, creativity, and production.

- Make available a variety of pathways to learning that accommodate different intelligences and learning styles.

- Allow students to make choices and contribute to some of their learning experiences.

- Use methods that engage students in hands-on learning.

- Focus instruction on reasoning and problem solving rather than only on recall of facts.

- Foster peer collaboration and extensive interaction between students and teachers.

- Stimulate internal rather than external motivation.

- Feature a variety of teaching techniques, including demonstrations, small-group activities, peer tutoring, and individual work, in addition to occasional lectures.

- Support energetic and integrated learning aimed at exploring concepts and producing work that is guided by rigorous standards.

- Exhibit a strong commitment to finding and implementing practices that respond to a wide range of individual differences.

In isolation from each other, these successful teaching strategies certainly are nothing new to many educators; however, we have often not practiced them all because of scarce resources and the inability of teachers to feel safe changing their instruction.

More specifically, many educators are beginning to implement ways to differentiate curriculum for all students (Tomlinson, 1999). We agree with Tomlinson (1999) that "to ensure maximum student growth, teachers need to make modifications for students rather than assume students must modify themselves to fit the curriculum. In fact, children do not know how to differentiate their own curriculum successfully" (p. 24). Although describing explicitly differentiated instruction is beyond the scope of this chapter, we refer the reader to two resources on the reference list: Tomlinson (1999) and Erikson (1998).

Standard 6:
Make Curriculum Accommodations but Not as a Substitute for Skillful Teaching

We have been impressed with the variety of resource guides and workshops that have created lists and processes for teachers to use in accommodating their instruction and curriculum to meet the needs of all their students (e.g., Ford et al., 1996). Because of these accommodations, hundreds of thousands of students have been able to participate fully in general education when, without accommodations, they otherwise would have be relegated to separate programs.

Accommodations should not be used as a substitute for skillful teaching, however. That is, we have witnessed students who have not received quality teaching in the first place and thus are lagging in skills. The "remedy" then is to make accommodations for this student in the curriculum and instruction and in some ways lower expectations for that student to acquire the skills. In so doing, the accommodations can result in enabling students and teachers. They can enable students by not challenging them to complete work that is more in line with their capabilities. They can enable teachers not to make changes in the curriculum and instruction in two ways: (a) not to examine how the curriculum and instruction could have prevented the student from not learning the skill or knowledge in the first place and (b) not to explore how they can differentiate the current instructional situation to meet all student needs. Accommodations imply that we prescribe a set curriculum and instruction to all the class, and then for those students who struggle with it, we make accommodations. These accommodations often take time to develop, can consume financial resources, and sometimes draw unnecessary negative attention to the students. Again, in this scenario, we blame students for not achieving and thus requiring accommodations. We would much rather see high-quality instruction that employs differentiated instruction for all students. Tomlinson (1999) agrees:

> Classrooms grounded in best-practice education, and modified to be responsive to student differences, benefit virtually all students. Differentiation addresses the needs of struggling and advanced learners. It addresses the needs of students for whom English is a second language and students who have strong learning style preferences. It addresses gender differences and cultural differences. It pays homage to the truth that we are not born to become replicas of one another. (p. 24)

For example, we worked with one student who, in kindergarten and the beginning of first grade, struggled with writing. This student had great difficulty forming letters correctly and matching letters to their sounds in spelling, and the entire process was slow, laborious, and frustrating to the student. The school identified his needs (without formal testing or labels) and quickly moved to include him in a small group that met in the classroom for 10 to 15 minutes daily and, in part, presented a structured, sequential, positive, child-centered, multisensory curriculum that included, for example, how to hold a pencil and how to form letters paired with their sounds. Within months, his writing had improved dramatically. In second grade, not only was his handwriting among the best in the class, but he eagerly wrote in his journal and felt very proud of his writing.

Another option could have been to conclude in first grade that this student was learning disabled or another label, seek to get him "qualified" for services, and then make accommodations for him, such as cutting down his writing assignments or obtaining a laptop computer for him to write with instead—in short, lower our expectations. If educators spent half as much time focusing on high-quality instruction as they often do referring, labeling, and accommodating students, schools and their students and staff might be far better off.

Standard 7: Use Teaching Assistants With Caution

As a first step toward including each student, districts often hire additional teaching assistants to support teachers. This practice can lead to teacher and student dependence on assistants and to much higher educational costs and can impede curriculum development. For example, one teacher said to us, "I have 20 kids, but I have this one kid who's very difficult. I spent an hour and a half with him." This student presented challenges. The teacher did not design her curriculum and instruction to address the variety of learning needs in her classroom, however, and the student was frustrated. This teacher should receive support. This teacher should not be assigned an educational assistant, though, just because the student is frustrated as a result of an inadequate curriculum and instruction. This teacher should be encouraged and supported (e.g., time off to learn about additional strategies, direct support from other teachers who accommodate diverse learners) to learn about differentiated instruction and other strategies to meet the diverse array of student needs in the classroom.

Therefore, do not hire teaching assistants as a remedy for ineffective teaching. Also, if an assistant is hired, with rare exception be sure the assistant is assigned to a class or grade with the expectation that he or she is to provide extra support for all the students in the class, not just for one particular student.

Standard 8: Begin With the End in Mind

With all effective teaching, we need to begin with the end in mind for each student, and a creative use of the standards in teaching can help us achieve that goal. Whether a student is 16 years old and is practicing pre-reading skills or whether a student has easily mastered all the high school standards by eighth grade, we need to ask, Where should this student be when he or she graduates? What can the district/school do to ensure that this student is a valuable, contributing member of society? and How can we maximize this student's strengths?

In sum, we believe that these eight standards for teaching can help pave the way for student success. Nevertheless, how do we know that students have been successful? In Chapter 10, we discuss how standards-based assessments not only can show whether students have been successful but also can serve as a key support for effective instruction.

Additional Resources

Snow, C. E., Burns, M. S., & Griffin, P. (Eds.). (1998). *Preventing reading difficulties in young children.* Washington, DC: National Academy Press. (1-800-624-6242)

Project Read, Bloomington, MN (1-800-450-0343), http://www.projectread.com

HANDOUT 9.1. Eight Standards for Teaching to Ensure Success

1. Reduce student-to-teacher ratios.

2. Make early literacy a priority.

3. Provide early intervention and prevention without labeling.

4. Configure class grouping to meet student needs without labeling.

5. Ensure that all students have access to quality teaching.

6. Make curriculum accommodations but not as a substitute for skillful teaching.

7. Use teaching assistants with caution.

8. Begin with the end in mind.

HANDOUT 9.2.
Possible Reading Options for Success for All Students
Can Take Place in Whole-Class or Small-Group Instruction

1. Whole language approaches only

2. Whole language combined with general instruction phonics
   (e.g., Reading Recovery)

3. General instruction phonics only

4. Whole language instruction combined with structured,
   sequential, direct instruction in phonics (e.g., Project Read)

5. Specific direct instruction in phonics only
   (e.g., direct instruction)

Colleen A. Capper, Elise Frattura, Maureen W. Keyes, *Meeting the Needs of Students of ALL Abilities: How Leaders Go Beyond Inclusion.* Copyright © 2000, Corwin Press, Inc.

HANDOUT 9.3. Successful Teaching Strategies

- Offer students challenging, interesting activities and rich materials for learning that foster thinking, creativity, and production.

- Make available a variety of pathways to learning that accommodates different intelligences and learning styles.

- Allow students to make choices and contribute to some of their learning experiences.

- Use methods that engage students in hands-on learning.

- Focus instruction on reasoning and problem solving rather than only on recall of facts.

- Foster peer collaboration and extensive interaction between students and teachers.

- Stimulate internal rather than external motivation.

- Feature a variety of teaching techniques, including demonstrations, small-group activities, peer tutoring, and individual work, in addition to occasional lectures.

- Support energetic and integrated learning aimed at exploring concepts and producing work that is guided by rigorous standards.

- Exhibit a strong commitment to finding and implementing practices that respond to a wide range of individual differences.

SOURCE: Adapted from Darling-Hammond and Falk (1997).

Self-Evaluation:
Leading Beyond Inclusion

Directions: Complete the following Likert-type scale by rating the level of success, as well as delineating strengths/limitations, the next steps that should be taken, and what the timeline might look like.

5 = How we do business;   4 = Increased comfort level;   3 = Beginning implementation;
2 = Emerging through conversation;   1 = Yet to acknowledge as a need

Focus Area Chapter 9: Standards-Based Teaching That Ensures Success	Likert-type Scale	Strengths/Limitations	Next Steps	Timeline
Major area of emphasis:				
1. Student-to-teacher ratios are being reduced with creative use of staff.	5 4 3 2 1			
2. Early literacy is a priority.	5 4 3 2 1			
3. All students have access to a variety of reading options.	5 4 3 2 1			
4. All preK-8 teachers and high school teachers who teach reading are reading experts.	5 4 3 2 1			
5. School administrators are familiar with various reading approaches and ensure that all teachers are skilled teachers of reading.	5 4 3 2 1			
6. Phonemic awareness is included in the kindergarten curriculum.	5 4 3 2 1			

7. Early intervention and prevention are provided without labeling.	5 4 3 2 1	
8. Classrooms are configured to meet individual student needs without labeling.	5 4 3 2 1	
9. All students have access to quality teaching.	5 4 3 2 1	
10. Curriculum modifications are not made as a substitute for skillful teaching.	5 4 3 2 1	
11. Teaching assistants are used with caution.	5 4 3 2 1	
12. We do not wait for students to fail before addressing their needs.	5 4 3 2 1	
13. Teachers begin with the end in mind.	5 4 3 2 1	

Comments:

Colleen A. Capper, Elise Frattura, Maureen W. Keyes, *Meeting the Needs of Students of ALL Abilities: How Leaders Go Beyond Inclusion.* Copyright © 2000, Corwin Press, Inc.

Chapter 10

Standards-Based Assessment to Ensure Student Success

We must assess students in a variety of ways (see Handout 10.1); that is, teachers must measure student performance by using a range of instruments and their own observation and professional judgment. In this chapter, we discuss standardized, performance-based, functional, and individualized assessment practices and identify their benefits and limitations (see Handout 10.2).

Standardized Assessments

A *standardized assessment* or test typically measures cognitive skills. Developers have systematically constructed these tests and expected them to be administered to all students with the same directions, questions, and time limits. Most standardized tests are multiple choice; however, open-ended questions have recently been added to some exams. Beginning with the Stanford Binet in the 1920s, such tests were initially used to exclude individuals from the military and educational settings. Thankfully, the normative sample that test publishers use to validate their tests' results and the ability to generalize across a vast segment of the population have evolved over time. Clearly, however, such assessment practices are currently not bias-free assessment measures even today.

The Federal Code of Regulations, during the reauthorization of the Individuals with Disabilities Educational Act (IDEA) in April 1997, clarified the requirement and responsibility of educators to include students with disabilities in standardized state and district assessment procedures. These regulations specifically require that children labeled with disabilities must

§300.347 3(iii) Be educated and participate with other children with disabilities and nondisabled children in the activities described in this paragraph:

(4) An explanation of the extent, if any, to which the child will not participate with nondisabled children in the regular class.

(5)(i) A statement of any individual modifications in the administration of state or district-wide assessments of student achievement that are needed in order for the child to participate in the assessment.

(ii) If the Individualized Educational Plan (IEP) team determines that the child will not participate in a particular state or district-wide assessment of student achievement (or part of an assessment), a statement of why the assessment is not appropriate for the child and how the child will be assessed is necessary.

We should apply these regulations to each student, not just to students labeled with disabilities (see Chapter 13 for further explanation).

Thurlow, Elliott, and Ysseldyke (1998, p. 13) list six reasons for including all students in district and state accountability practices:

1. Students are more likely to benefit from instructional changes and educational reforms when they are included in the accountability system.

2. New legislation requires their participation.

3. Students need to gain skills involved in taking tests.

4. The possibility of corruption is reduced when all students are included in the accountability system.

5. Participation in the accountability system provides an avenue for program monitoring and evaluation.

6. Most students with disabilities have mild disabilities and should be pursuing the same educational goals as other students: these students should be taking the same assessments either with or without accommodations.

Students who challenge schools the most are the ones affected the most by our inability to assess in a way that shows their true abilities. In some school districts, as many as 38% of students are withheld from state and district standardized assessment practices. Students are typically withheld because of the inability of educators to offer appropriate modifications for small groups of students or on an individualized scale. We must work toward including each student in standardized assessments.

Performance-Based Assessments

Performance-based assessment teaches us what a child knows and how the child learns within the environment where we give the assessment. We should offer assessment in a variety of formats and environments. These include portfolio assessments, performance exams, exhibitions, parent conferences, school report cards, and school quality review teams (Peterson & Neill, 1999). Here, we describe the most common: portfolio assessments and performance exams.

With *portfolio assessments,* student work is collected over a period to show student progress. Advantages include the fact that

> the evaluation is based on a wide range of student work done over a long period of time, rather than a single paper-and-pencil test taken over a few hours. . . . It encourages districts to invest in the professional development of teachers, and it pushes teachers to reflect more consistently on the quality of student work in their classroom. (Peterson & Neill, 1999, p. 4)

It can also encourage collaboration among teachers. Problems include the logistics of storing portfolios, its dependence on quality teachers, its overreliance on the judgment of individual teachers, and the ways it can drive the curriculum.

Performance exams are "tests given to all students, based on students performing a certain task, such as writing an essay, conducting a science experiment, or doing an oral presentation which is videotaped" (Peterson & Neill, 1999, p. 5). These exams actively involve students in hands-on learning. Like other alternative tests, these exams can take extensive teacher and student time and resources. Performance-based assessments can also be prone to similar problems as standardized assessments: "inequity, inadequacy, and subjectivity" (Peterson & Neill, 1999, p. 28).

Functional Assessments

Brown et al. (1979) believed that we should not use standardized assessments for students with severe intellectual disabilities. The tests were inappropriate for these students for two reasons. First, developers did not norm these instruments for students with severe disabilities; therefore, we were comparing these students with a population unlike them. Second, these assessments did not provide any useful information to the teacher. Results of these assessments were general measures and did not provide specific information about these students' skills, strengths, or needs or how these students learned.

For example, standardized instruments for students with severe disabilities could assign a 15-year-old a 9-month level in language skills, leaving families and school personnel wondering what to teach. Should the teacher just care for the student and not expect any skill acquisition, or should the teacher teach skills and provide activities that might be developmentally appropriate for a 9-month-old but terribly inappropriate for a 15-year-old (e.g., teaching the student how to manipulate a baby's busy box)?

Such testing resulted in the institutionalization of many students with severe disabilities, the treatment of young adults as if they were infants, and an overall quality of life that left them stuck in an infant stage. Because of these results, Brown developed a functional assessment discrepancy analysis. This analysis assessed the functional skills a child was able and not able to do—skills that would enhance the child's independence and quality of life based on her or his chronological age. For example, typical 15-year-olds know how to activate a CD player with headphones and how to make their own beds. We compared the skills the student could do against a list of skills that would enhance the student's independence and quality of life. The discrepancy between what the student could do and the skills that would enhance her or his independence became the student's goals. These skills were concrete and practical. A teacher could easily create lesson plans based on this analysis.

Over the past 20 years, educators have used these functional assessments primarily for students with severe intellectual disabilities in recreation, community, domestic, and vocational environments. The reauthorization of IDEA in 1997 requires educators to use a "functional behavioral assessment and implement a behavioral intervention plan" to support students who exhibit high behavioral needs or challenging behaviors within the school environment before the student's behavior results in suspension or pending expulsion. Because of this regulation, many experts have developed detailed questionnaires to assist teachers in deciding how the student was functioning within her or his current environment before the challenging behaviors. These questionnaires are completed before the student can be placed in a more restrictive environment.

Unfortunately, although functional assessments have been available to educators for more than two decades and have been revived because of IDEA, many educators have limited the use of functional assessments only to those students involved in suspension and expulsion proceedings. We advocate the use of functional assessments as another assessment tool for all students.

A functional assessment can be used as a proactive approach for learners who do not follow the building discipline plan, have a behavioral or social disability, or are receiving vocational instruction or functional curriculum in the community. Such an approach to assessment allows educators to determine the discrepancies of the child and to focus on goals for learning that can be applied to the standards, curriculum, and assessment template (see Chapter 8).

Handout 10.3 is a functional inventory and assessment process format. The format requires educators, along with the student and family members, to determine the day and time of day when the student struggles in some way; identify the environments where students without labels are present; describe the activities and behaviors/skills elicited by a same-age peer throughout the day; identify areas of concern in relation to age-appropriate behaviors; recommend specific student behaviors based on previous antecedents and other consequences applied; and outline teacher behaviors to assist in the implementation of learning. After completion of a functional analysis in the area of behavior of a student, we can then develop a behavioral protocol (see Chapter 11 for student behavioral protocol information).

Individualized Assessments

After students fail in an academic area, we often assess them with a variety of isolated assessment tools associated with specific federal and district programs—for example, Title I, Section 504, English as a second language (ESL), or alcohol and other drug abuse programs (AODA). These assessments are often disjointed and reactionary. Further, for students who are failing in some way, most educators (because of federal laws) first assume for which special program the students may qualify (e.g., special education, 504, Title I). Then, on the basis of this assumption, we assess the students with instruments and procedures that special programs require. Each program has different instruments and procedures. Parents usually understand that schools can offer a range of services dependent on their child's needs. What does not make sense, however, is the need to complete many different assessment forms dependent on the presumed area of need.

For example, we have required students and families to complete a reading assessment, followed by a Section 504 assessment, only finally to be assessed in the area of special education. We remove students from their classrooms for each assessment. Thus students who require consistent instruction with minimal transitions are the students we remove from the education environment most frequently for assessments.

We should not require educators to decide which assessment procedure to use: special education? Section 504? AODA? Title I? Reading or math? The assessment process should not be differentiated by federal regulations and entitlement dollars at the local level. One assessment process should suffice and allow for a seamless procedure for students, teachers, and parents. In so doing, stigmatizing program areas would play less of a role.

If we offer students a differentiated curriculum and a range of assessment options (from standard to performance-based to functional assessment) and we are not meeting their needs, then an individualized analysis of student learning is needed. That is, teachers, students, and family members may need additional information from individualized assessments to determine how students learn (vs. what they know). Rather than the fragmented, disjointed procedures of program-based assessments, we need to determine exactly what additional information we need for effective teaching. We can obtain this information through a variety of assessments, gathering only the data we need.

A Proactive Assessment Process in a Context of Belonging

To move from a reactive, inefficient, stigmatizing assessment process that segregates students to one that is inclusive and proactive, we can rely on the reauthorization of IDEA specifically in relation to assessment procedures and adapt these procedures for all students. With these inclusive procedures, the parent, teacher, and student can cooperatively complete a referral. On receipt, a preassessment meeting determines exactly what data are currently available in the student's portfolio and what additional data are necessary to help meet this student's needs. What would be the most efficient, proactive way to gather these data? From the menu of assessment choices, which make the most sense?

Following this data gathering, we can hold findings meetings to discuss the results of the assessment and to determine appropriate standards and goals for the student. After writing the goals and objectives, the district confirms that it will provide the services. In this way, we provide student services based on identified needs rather than on segregated funding arrangements and programs. If the student meets eligibility for any specific service areas, the standards, curriculum, and assessment template then becomes the service plan incorporating progress to date on the standards. Additional pages may be added for functional skills, processing needs, or other areas currently not included in the student assessment and standards portfolio.

Although standards for curriculum, teaching, and assessment are crucial, students with challenging behaviors often baffle educators. We often view these students as impediments to the academic culture of schools. Therefore, in Chapter 11 we outline standards for student behavior.

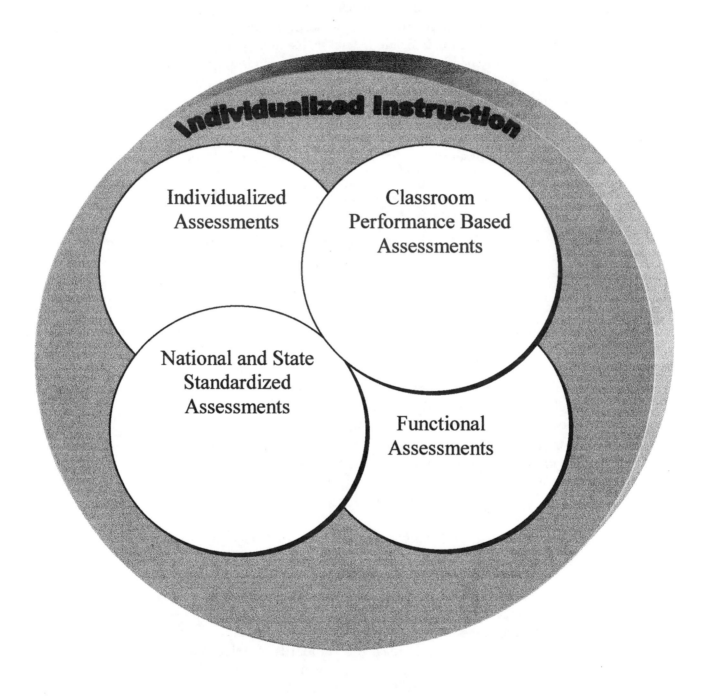

Colleen A. Capper, Elise Frattura, Maureen W. Keyes, *Meeting the Needs of Students of ALL Abilities: How Leaders Go Beyond Inclusion.* Copyright © 2000, Corwin Press, Inc.

HANDOUT 10.2. Benefits and Limitations of Assessments: Standardized, Performance-Based, Functional, and Individualized

Types of Assessment	Benefits of the Assessments	Limitations of the Assessments
Standardized assessment practices	• Time efficient • Availability of local, state, and national comparisons • Significant amount of quantitative data • State-standardized assessments presume to provide accountability • Forces discussion around teaching and learning	• Snapshot • One way of showing a student's ability • Not longitudinal in nature • May not be the best method for students to demonstrate what they know • Minimizes nontested areas • May heighten a student's test anxiety
Performance-based assessment practices	• Criterion-reference-based • Shows students' "in-context work" • Assessment is timely with the information presented • Brings ease to monitoring individual student growth • Back-mapped from the standards	• Subjective • Time consuming • Storage of materials (portfolios) • Validity • Cost on large scale
Functional assessment practices	• Individually based • May be proactive to determine more intricate needs • Often links directly to an intervention • Provides a positive vision for students • Solution oriented • Highlights strengths	• Limited to one student at a time • Time intensive • Appropriate analysis of data and solutions may be time intensive
Individualized assessment practices	• Multiple data options • Allows for greater insight about an individual learner's learning style, physical needs, processing abilities, etc. • Leads directly to areas of necessary interventions	• May be held to normative expectations that are not normed on a similar population • Time intensive

HANDOUT 10.3. Functional Assessment

Student: Tammy (15 years old)

Day and time	Functional age expectations Environment/Activity Behavior/Skill (Delineate those typical environments, activities, and behaviors/skills elicited by a peer throughout the three main blocks of the day)	Assessment of needs (Delineate areas of concern in comparing the student's behavior to the expectations listed)	Recommended student goals and objectives (Focus on those goals that would lend themselves toward the expectation stated in the second column)	Teacher response (On the basis of the recommended goals and objectives, delineate methodology or what the teacher will do to teach to the recommended goals)
Early morning	• Awake on time • Eat breakfast • Groom • Get ready for school • Catch the bus • Arrive to school on time • Arrive first hour on time	• Wakes up late • Doesn't eat • Grooms and gets ready for school • Arrives late • Misses first hour	• Purchases an alarm and learns how to set it for the appropriate time • Arrives at school with an arranged peer • First hour arranged with support staff to organize homework and purchase breakfast	• Teacher provides community support to purchase an alarm. • Teacher provides first-hour support. • Teacher provides functional, hands-on examples for assignments.
School hours	• Attend classes • Follow directions in class • Gather homework assignments • Socialize with peers • Plan for evening activities • Enjoy lunch with friends • Purchase lunch • Leave school on time with needed homework materials • Catch bus	• Skips second hour to get something to eat with friends • Arrives late for third hour • Sleeps through class • Takes off with friends fourth hour • Returns with friends sixth hour and ends up in the principal's office for skipping	• Tammy will take classes that will assist her to be more self-reliant and successful as an adult—Foods, Weight Lifting, School to Work, Health and Wellness.	• Guidance counselor will organize schedule changes. • Staff will meet to determine how best to meet Tammy's needs within integrated school environments by using a functional/hands-on curriculum approach.
After school/ Early evening	• Begins homework • Meet friends at the mall • Return home for dinner • Assist in cleanup • Finish homework • Groom and prepare for bed • Set alarm for morning	• Does not bring homework home, does not know what homework she has to do • Does not go home, hangs out on the streets • Arrives home at midnight • Eats junk food and falls asleep around 2 a.m.	• Tammy will get a job in her area of interest. • Tammy will expand her healthy recreational options. • Tammy will learn how to manage her finances.	• Staff will assist Tammy in applying for and finding a job in her area of interest. • Staff will assist Tammy in attending a "drug-free" support group. • Staff will assist Tammy in joining the after-school weight-lifting club.

Colleen A. Capper, Elise Frattura, Maureen W. Keyes, Meeting the Needs of Students of ALL Abilities: How Leaders Go Beyond Inclusion. Copyright © 2000, Corwin Press, Inc.

Self-Evaluation:
Leading Beyond Inclusion

Directions: Complete the following Likert-type scale by rating the level of success, as well as delineating strengths/limitations, the next steps that should be taken, and what the timeline might look like.

5 = How we do business;   4 = Increased comfort level;   3 = Beginning implementation;
2 = Emerging through conversation;   1 = Yet to acknowledge as a need

Focus Area Chapter 10: Standards-Based Assessment to Ensure Student Success	Likert-type Scale	Strengths/ Limitations	Next Steps	Timeline
Major area of emphasis:				
1. A multifaceted assessment process is used to measure student performance in ways that students may demonstrate their knowledge/skills.	5 4 3 2 1			
2. Teachers have the ability to measure the student's performance against standards through a multifaceted assessment process.	5 4 3 2 1			
3. Standardized assessments are used for all students to link to individually appropriate standards.	5 4 3 2 1			
4. We include all students in standards-based assessments.	5 4 3 2 1			
5. Performance-based assessments are used for all students to link to individually appropriate standards.	5 4 3 2 1			
6. Functional assessments are used for all students, not just for students with challenging behaviors.	5 4 3 2 1			

(Continued)

Self-Evaluation *(Continued)*

5 = How we do business;   4 = Increased comfort level;   3 = Beginning implementation;
2 = Emerging through conversation;   1 = Yet to acknowledge as a need

Focus Area Chapter 10: Standards-Based Assessment to Ensure Student Success	Likert-type Scale	Strengths/ Limitations	Next Steps	Timeline
7. We do not require educators or families to receive separate assessments from separate programs (e.g., Title I, special education).	5 4 3 2 1			
8. We only gather the data we need about students to make curriculum decisions; we do not require students to be assessed in areas that are not necessary.	5 4 3 2 1			
9. Our data gathering includes a thorough identification of the student's gifts and strengths.	5 4 3 2 1			
10. When we hold meetings to discuss students, we give equal attention to strengths as well as needs.	5 4 3 2 1			
11. We use an individual assessment process for all students to link to individually appropriate standards.	5 4 3 2 1			

Comments:

Colleen A. Capper, Elise Frattura, Maureen W. Keyes, *Meeting the Needs of Students of ALL Abilities: How Leaders Go Beyond Inclusion.* Copyright © 2000, Corwin Press, Inc.

Chapter 11

Standards for Student Behavior

Some educators believe that one of the greatest challenges to creating and sustaining schools that work for all students is working with troubled and troubling students. Strategies and supports that we often suggest for students with challenging behaviors, however, should not be reserved for students with these needs. All students should have access to, and can benefit from, these strategies and supports. For example, providing adult mentors, collaborating with community agencies to support the students and their families, providing effective instruction to prevent student frustration, teaching responsibility, involving students in problem solving around their needs, teaching students how to handle intense feelings, teaching anger management, and detracking schools that enable all students to have opportunities for a challenging and interesting curriculum are all strategies and supports that would benefit all students in the school. Similar to students with learning challenges, from our experience and the research, we believe evidence is scant that students who challenge the system need supports radically different from those of other students, although they may need much more intensive support. In this chapter, we identify nine standards that suggest ways to provide more intensive support coupled with high expectations for student behavior (see Handout 11.1). As a reminder, we can apply all these standards to all students, not just to students who challenge the system in some way.

Standard 1:
Be Conscious of How We Label Students;
Student Behavior Is Relative

According to Villa, Udis, and Thousand (1994), the way we view and, in turn, "name" or label students who are troubled or troubling determines how we approach these students. Villa et al. explain:

For a variety of administrative, fiscal, legal, educational, and theoretical reasons, many different labels . . . have been developed and attached to students who appear troubled or troubling in school. Labels include emotionally disturbed, disruptive, delinquent, acting out, unmanageable, conduct disordered, socially maladjusted, anti-social, noncompliant, and serious behavior problems. . . . [We add to this list, hyperactive, ADD, ADHD.] Regardless of the origins of these labels and definitions, they all have an extraordinary impact upon the children to whom they are applied. (p. 370)

Villa et al. (1994) further explain that "what gets labeled as a *serious* behavior problem . . . varies from one school to the next and from class to class" (p. 370). This variability depends on "a community's beliefs about and successes (or failures) with [these students]" (p. 370). For example, given a challenging student, some educators would respond with "exclusion, expulsion, or restrictive placement outside of general education" (p. 370). Others would respond with providing extra structure in the classroom and additional support services. They would couple these strategies with an intensive inquiry into efforts the school may have made to prevent such behaviors, going back to a student's earliest grades in school. They would conduct this inquiry not only to address this student's immediate needs but also as a way to address the needs of students in the future.

The language we prefer to use to refer to students who challenge the system is "students with challenging behaviors." Villa et al. (1994) also use the terms *"children who are troubled or troubling, students who are challenged or challenging, children who demonstrate high rates of rule-violating behavior, or students who have acquired nonadaptive ways of relating"* (p. 370).

In addition, like our premise throughout this book, we view troubled and troubling students on a continuum, and all of us—students and adults—at least occasionally feel troubled or challenge systems in some way. Rather than always viewing these students as "other" and different and separate from us, we can identify the ways we are similar and with similar basic needs. In so doing, we should never blame families for their children's behavioral challenges. According to Villa et al. (1994), "Parents and families are central to solution-finding processes; the responsibility of educators is to work with and for families rather than blame them or their child for their troubles" (p. 373).

Standard 2: Hold High Expectations for Student Behavior in a Context of Care

Congruent with our assumptions in other chapters, we must give equal attention to high expectations for student behavior coupled with intensive and consistent support and care. High expectations without support and care result in student frustration, failure, and blaming the student and the student's parents. High support and empathy with students who are challenging without high expectations result in mediocrity and, ironically, lower self-esteem in students.

Standard 3: Develop and Consistently Implement Schoolwide Discipline Policies That Have Individually Designed Consequences

In typical schools, approximately 85% of the student body respond well to current guidelines for behavior and discipline that are located in the context of a challenging curriculum, instruction gauged to student learning needs, and a culture of belonging and community (Taylor-Greene et al., 1997). Addressing student behavioral needs should not be an add-on program and should be woven into the fabric of the school. Separate initiatives do not work and are only short-term solutions.

Brendtro, Brokenleg, and Van Bockern (1990), in their significant work titled *Reclaiming Youth at Risk: Our Hope for the Future,* describe the importance of nurturing students' needs in the areas of independence, belonging, generosity, and mastery. We would add another component, dignity for the spirit, to the authors' framework because of the crucial role a student's spiritual core plays in developing a successful educational experience. For example, when the discipline procedures and efforts of staff and students are unsuccessful, the unmet needs of a student are pervasive, negatively affecting the student's spirit.

The framework illustrates students' needs to (a) master content and material to gain academic skills, (b) express their gifts and talents to give generously to both self and others, (c) belong within the school community, (d) develop their sense of independence as they grow and mature, and (e) reveal their spiritual identities within an atmosphere laced with dignity and respect. This framework should serve as a guide for all students.

A schoolwide discipline policy should support this framework; that is, the same high expectations for student behavior should apply to all students. We must individualize consequences for challenging behavior, however, on the basis of student needs. We list in Handout 11.2 some practical schoolwide strategies to which at least 85% of students respond.

Standard 4: Provide Early Intervention

Paralleling other ideas in this book, being successful with students who challenge the system requires early intervention. Most educators are ill-prepared to address positively student behavioral challenges.

Even educators certified to work with students who have challenging behaviors are not always fully prepared for the variety of situations they will encounter in schools. University education programs contribute to this poor preparation by not adequately addressing these issues.

As a result, our experience suggests that schools often do not provide a curriculum, instruction, and classroom culture that can prevent student frustration that often results in behavioral challenges. Further, educators tend to ignore student misbehavior or to apply behavioral bandages, hoping the behavior will subside. Only when student behavior reaches crisis proportions do schools begin to respond in a systematic way, usually through suspension and expulsion. By this time, hope for lasting student change dims.

Further, regardless of when educators respond, rarely do schools respond to a student who challenges the system by looking at itself to determine in what ways the school could have contributed to the student's condition. Where, in the student's educational experience, did he or she first begin struggling with school? What was the school's response? Was the school's response effective? What seemed to work, and what did not? What can the school do in the future to be more helpful? Similar to academic needs, to wait to support students until the student meets the eligibility requirement for special education services is too late.

Schools that are successful with all students plan to prevent challenging behaviors by building relationships. Student respect and learning responsibility can only occur in positive relationships with adults. We can strengthen adult-student relationships by getting to know the student, identifying the student's strengths, needs, goals, family goals, student's history, and teaching methods and styles that are successful.

Standard 5: Involve Students in All Aspects of Intervention

Students who challenge the system can be our best teachers. They must be integrally involved in planning and problem solving on their behalf. Students with the most challenging behaviors are often quite clever and could, as a consequence for their misbehavior, be responsible for helping develop more responsive plans for either themselves or others. These students, like all students, should always attend their own IEP meetings and other meetings held to problem-solve on their behalf.

Standard 6: All Staff Must Understand That All Behavior Is an Attempt to Communicate

Students respond in particular ways, depending on the communicative intent of their behavior. This means that one of the first questions educators need to ask themselves when a student's behavior challenges existing norms is, What is the student trying to communicate with this behavior? Possible explanations for challenging behaviors include a student's need for revenge, power, control, escape or avoidance, self-regulation, play, attention, and coping. We need to identify the motivation behind each student's expression of challenging behavior. In so doing, we can develop responsive, individual plans to help the student learn new, more appropriate ways to interact with the environment.

For example, behavioral support plans for students seeking revenge ought to differ from those plans designed to help students with needs for attention, play, or entertainment. A student seeking revenge toward another student may need to be kept away from the other student while he or she has the opportunity to explore his or her emotions in a supportive manner. Merely to suspend students for threatening another does nothing to consider the communicative intent behind their behavior. If a student wants to get even with another student for a specific reason, punishment will not avert this situation; it will merely postpone it (see Handout 11.3 for common behaviors associated with each communication category).

Students with challenging behaviors are responding to the environment in the best manner they know—albeit irritating and disconcerting at times to other school staff and possibly their peers. When developing responsive plans for students' behaviors, we need to recognize that the students are expressing a need for more than just a consequence for their actions. Often, students with quick retorts and hurtful comments toward staff and peers are searching for a way to belong and, with no other known recourse, have chosen to lash out or make fun of those either in power or in the teachers' good graces.

Understanding the communicative intent of behavior, however, does not excuse the behavior. Rather, this understanding helps educators develop support plans that can match the intent of the behavior.

Standard 7: All Staff Must Have Similar Expectations and Strategies for Student Behavior

During the early phases of exploring students' behavior, we need to interview or survey the adults in the students' lives to secure information describing the most successful and the most ineffective methods of obtaining positive behaviors in the students' performance within various environments. For example, if one teacher has no difficulty with a student's behavior in class, we need to study and duplicate this teacher's approach if possible. In the opposite situation, if the team supporting a student's behavior is reporting significant success but one teacher continues to experience difficulty, this staff member may not be following the established protocol for this student.

Another angle to consider when interviewing teachers is the significance of high expectations. For example, if one teacher reports no difficulty with a student's behavior and, on observation, a team member determines that the teacher puts no demands on the student in a particular environment, this is problematic as well. High expectations for positive behaviors by the focus student and consistent support in all environments provide a strong statement to the student, his or her peers, and the adults in the student's life that all members of his or her support team believe that the student can behave appropriately.

Standard 8: View Teaching and Learning Appropriate Behaviors as a Long-Term Process

Villa et al. (1994) describe the importance of viewing the learning of appropriate behaviors in the same way we view learning any other skill:

> When students fail to learn new skills or concepts, we respond by re-teaching the material, providing additional or different types of supports, and making accommodations. . . . Yet, . . . the content area known as "responsibility" . . . is relegated to "add-on" or "quick-fix" instructional methods (e.g., seeing the guidance counselor, attending a 6-week social skills group, making an oral or a written plan, talking about it after school). Furthermore, when a student demonstrates a lack of responsibility (frequently in the form of rule-violating behavior such as tardiness, verbal aggression, rudeness, and failure to follow instructions), we (the adults of the school)

often "take the behavior personally" and respond with an emotional, punishing response, rather than with an emotionally neutral teaching response. The teaching of responsibility is no less demanding a task than the teaching of any other curriculum area; it requires careful thought and reflection, complex instruction starting at the earliest ages and continuing throughout the school years, and patience. (p. 375)

We see educators' frustrations and lack of understanding that some students need to be taught and to learn appropriate behaviors in the same way these students need to be taught and to learn algebra or world history. Unfortunately, some school policies and practices ignore this fact. For example, some schools award field trips or class parties or other incentives for students who "follow" school rules and do not have any behavioral infractions. We do not oppose all behavioral incentives, but we call these types of reinforcements "big bang rewards." These large rewards that accrue over time assume that the only reason a student struggles with behavior is that he or she is not motivated enough. Therefore, if a school offers a high, external incentive, then the student will not challenge the system.

If this assumption were true, then educators could require all students in the school to achieve a score of 1,200 on the SAT and then award a free trip to an amusement park to all who do. The assumption is that all students can score 1,200. Nevertheless, educators know that, for some students, no matter how enticing the reward and no matter how seriously the students focus on achieving the goal, some students will never receive 1,200. The message that educators send to students who do not earn the big bang reward, however, is that these students did not try hard enough and it is the student's fault for not achieving the reward. Incentive programs such as these further wither students' self-esteem and discourage positive relationships with others.

Similarly, educators should typically not withhold recess from students who do not complete their work satisfactorily or who misbehave. Usually, these students need the gross motor play and freedom offered by recess, not as an "extra" part of their day, but as necessary for them to do their best work. Just as we need to tailor consequences for students individually, we need to do the same with rewards.

Standard 9: Staff Must Use Proactive Strategies for Students Who Need More Intense Support

Schoolwide curriculum, instruction, culture, and discipline plans address the behavioral needs of 85% of students. The remaining 15% of the student body do not respond consistently to schoolwide guidelines for behavior and discipline. Therefore, as faculty strive to reach the unmet needs of this 15%, they often deplete their energies for those students willing to follow the expectations. Consequently, as staff struggle to meet not only the unique needs of the 15% but the majority as well, their frustrations grow, and justifiably so. Within this 15% of students who inconsistently respond to general discipline and procedural guidelines, approximately 10% respond more positively with minor alterations in the existing program (e.g., more parent contact, application of natural consequences for infractions). With these students, additional supports may be necessary (see Handout 11.4).

Of the remaining 5%, approximately 4% are the student population labeled with emotional or behavioral difficulties.[1] In addition to schoolwide behavioral support and intense behavioral support in a context of high expectations, we need to take an even more structured approach to ensure that we meet these students' needs. Such an approach must involve the primary individuals in the student's life to complete a functional behavioral assessment and behavioral plan (see Handouts 11.5 through 11.7 for examples).

A proliferation of functional behavioral assessments are on the market now. We have found, however, several key aspects to make a difference for the 4% of students who may need more consistent structure and response to their behaviors.

Identify the Student's Positive Behaviors and Strengths. All students, regardless of their challenging behaviors, have many strengths and gifts. Most often in student meetings, however, we focus only on problems. Specifically writing down student strengths and positive student behaviors can help us build on these strengths and behaviors when writing the behavior plan.

Focus on Just Three or Fewer Behaviors to Change. Although some students may have many behavioral challenges, with the individual student we need to prioritize and focus on just one to three behaviors we wish to change. The student cannot work on more changes than this, and adults cannot provide proactive, positive, and consistent support beyond this number of behaviors. By focusing on just a few behaviors, success is more likely for the student and the adults.

Determine Ground Rules for Success. At the top of the behavior plan (see Handout 11.6), list three to five supports (ground rules) the student needs to be successful with his or her behavior. Often, if we provide these simple supports consistently, we can prevent most challenging behaviors from occurring. These supports should be available to the student at all time in all classes. In the example in Handout 11.6, the ground rules include: (a) Sawyer needs time to process information, (b) the information needs to be presented visually and orally, and (c) the teacher needs to provide intermittent, positive reinforcement.

Describe Engagement in Work. Most behavioral protocols focus on the problem behavior. In Handout 11.6 in the first column under the heading *student behavior*, we should first identify how the student appears when engaged in work. Again, keep the description simple and to the point. For Sawyer, when he is engaged in work, he (a) is quiet, (b) is mindful, and (c) may stand up but will continue to be on task. Including this aspect also reminds us that most students are not engaged in challenging behavior all the time.

Describe Signs of Resolution. The last item in the student behavior column of Handout 11.6 should include a description of signs of resolution that characterize how the student's challenging behavior appears when it is de-escalating. For Sawyer, he is moving out of his challenging behavioral episode when he allows staff to walk with him, and he becomes more logical in his reasoning. Including this aspect in the plan reminds us that challenging behaviors do end and pass over time.

Determine Initial and Follow-Up Adult Response. Most behavior plans identify what the student must do differently but fail to mention the role of adults in the plan. We identify what the initial adult response should be in response to Sawyer's behavior. If the behavior continues or escalates, then we identify a follow-up adult response. Identifying the specific adult response means that all adults in the student's environment can respond in a similar way to the student's challenging behavior, greatly increasing the possibility of preventing the behavior from escalating. In addition, if, for example, Sawyer begins hitting or kicking or tries to run from the school, a teacher can ask for backup support from the school office and quickly identify where the teacher and student are in the behavior plan. In this case, the teacher can simply say "I am at Behavior 3, Number 2." This lets the administrative support person know exactly what has already taken place with the student and adult responses and thus expedites the administrative support for the teacher and student.

In sum, standards for student behavior are crucial for achieving schools that meet the needs of all students. This concludes our suggestions in Part II for establishing a broad range of standards beyond the narrow perspectives often associated with standards initiatives. We examined in Part I how to move from programs to services. In Part III we show how the law and funding can further our efforts to meet the needs of students of all abilities.

Note

1. We credit Bill Conzemius for his idea of considering the 15% of the student population who may not respond to schoolwide behavioral strategies. Of the 15%, 10% respond to more intensive support, and 4% are students typically labeled with an emotional disability who receive more structured services via the IEP. In rare cases, less than 1% of students could be considered to have such severe emotional needs that they need support beyond the typical school environment. Often, educators categorize any students with challenging behaviors as those who must be removed from the school. We contend that students in this category are an overstated minority and that the standards outlined in this chapter can make significant differences in the behavior of all students over time.

HANDOUT 11.1. Standards for Student Behavior

Standard 1: Be conscious of how we label students; student behavior is relative.

Standard 2: Hold high expectations for student behavior in a context of care.

Standard 3: Develop and consistently implement schoolwide discipline policies that have individually designed consequences.

Standard 4: Provide early intervention.

Standard 5: Involve students in all aspects of interventions.

Standard 6: All staff must understand that all behavior is an attempt to communicate.

Standard 7: All staff must have similar expectations and strategies for student behavior.

Standard 8: View teaching and learning appropriate behaviors as a long-term process.

Standard 9: Staff must use proactive strategies for students who need more intense support.

HANDOUT 11.2. Schoolwide Strategies for Behavior

- Effective instruction and accommodations

- Classroom rules and consequences

- Prompts, reminders, and warnings

- Positive reinforcement (individual and group)

- Schoolwide discipline system

- Empowerment and choices in learning

- Basic needs met (e.g., belonging, self-esteem)

- Motivation through responsibility

- Responsive schedules

SOURCE: Adapted from Villa, R. (1998). *Creative Responses to Students Experiencing Behavioral and Emotional Challenges: From Risk to Resilience.* Presentation at the St. Louis Inclusion Conference. Used with permission.

HANDOUT 11.3.
Common Behaviors Associated With Each Communication Category

Attention	Escape/Avoidance	Control
Possible origins of behavior	*Possible origins of behavior*	*Possible origins of behavior*
Adults pay more attention to inappropriate than appropriate behaviors.	Unreasonable expectations by others.	Society stresses dominant-submissive roles rather than equality in relationships.
Student doesn't know how to ask for attention appropriately.	Student's belief that only perfection is acceptable; star mentality.	Success is defined as achieving personal power.
Student doesn't get sufficient personal attention.	Emphasis on competition in the classroom.	Lack of control in person's life.
Student has few friends.	Failure to be avoided at all costs.	Past history of abuse/victimization.
Student has low self-esteem.	The work is too difficult for the student.	
Student behavior	*Student behavior*	*Student behavior*
Behavior distracts teacher and classmates.	The student engages in the behavior when pressured to succeed.	When doing the behavior, the student is disruptive and confrontational.
Behavior occurs when no one is paying attention to the student.	The student procrastinates, fails to complete projects.	Quiet noncompliance; when doing the behavior, the student is often pleasant and even agreeable.
Behavior occurs when someone stops paying attention to the student.	The student develops a temporary incapacity or assumes behaviors that resemble a learning disability.	Behavior occurs when an activity or event is taken away.
Behavior occurs when attention is paid to someone other than the student.	The student develops physical complaints.	Behavior stops when student gets way.
Behavior occurs in front of valued peers.	Behavior occurs when the student is asked to do something he or she does not like to do.	
Behavior occurs as a dare or result of peer pressure.	Behavior stops after you stop making demands.	
	Behavior occurs in stressful situations.	

(Continued)

Revenge	Self-Regulation	Play
Possible origins of behavior	*Possible origins of behavior*	*Possible origins of behavior*
A reflection of the increasing violence in society.	Has not learned alternative ways of coping.	Society expects children to play: "Play is the work of children."
Media role models that solve conflicts by force.	Understimulated by environment.	The student is involved in routine, structured activities for long periods of time.
Unjust society; unequal treatment.	The student may be gifted, or experiencing a learning impairment, ADHD, or post-traumatic stress disorder.	Lack of opportunities to interact with peers.
Anger over personal circumstances or past "wrongs."		
Provocation by another.		
Jealousy.		
Student behavior	*Student behavior*	*Student behavior*
Behavior is hurtful.	Behavior tends to happen over and over again.	Behavior would occur when no one else was around.
The student is sullen and withdrawn, refusing overtures of friendship.	Attempts to reduce stimulation.	The student seems to enjoy performing the behavior.
The student does not show remorse following behavior.	Behavior occurs when a lot is going on.	The student is sorry if someone gets hurt.
Behavior occurs after you take something away.	The student can do other things while doing the behavior.	The student is reluctant to stop the behavior when asked to do so.
Behavior occurs after you require the student to do an unwanted activity.	Behavior tends to occur in stressful, anxiety-producing, or highly demanding situations.	
The student stops the behavior only when he or she wants.	Attempts to increase stimulation.	
The student expresses concerns about "fairness."	Behavior occurs when little is going on.	
Behavior is directed at person who is perceived as more "valued" by others.	Behavior occurs when the student seems bored.	
	Behavior seems to follow periods of nonactivity (e.g., periods of seat work).	

SOURCE: Topper, K., Williams, W., Leo, K., Hamilton, R., and Fox, T. (1994). Used with permission.

HANDOUT 11.4. More Intensive Behavioral Support

- Cues and self-monitoring techniques

- Positive practice

- Restitution

- Oral and written plans

- Redirection

- Direct teaching of interpersonal behaviors

- Time out from positive reinforcement

- Direct social skills instruction

- Anger management

- Impulse control strategies

SOURCE: Adapted from Thousand, J. S., Villa, R. A., and Nevin, A. I. (Eds.). (1994). *Creativity and Collaborative Learning: A Practical Guide to Empowering Students and Teachers* (pp. 369-390). Baltimore: Paul H. Brookes. Used with permission.

HANDOUT 11.5. Process for Functional Behavioral Assessment

Establish a collaborative team that includes the student, at least one student peer (if appropriate), sibling, and other family members important in the student's life.

1. List all positive or appropriate behaviors the student has and all his or her individual strengths. These behaviors can be classified under the multiple intelligences frames of interpersonal, intrapersonal, music, mathematics, linguistic, nature, humor, and spirit.

2. List all challenging behaviors in observable terms, communicative intent of behavior, frequency and duration of the behavior. Finally, describe the school's typical responses to the behavior and rate the behavior according to seriousness:

Behavior	Observable terms	Communicative intent (perceived purpose of behavior/history)	Frequency of behavior	Duration of behavior	What preceded behavior (e.g., time, places, with whom)	Typical response and outcome at school/at home	Rate by seriousness (e.g., distracting, disruptive, destructive)

3. Determine the top three behaviors that the team will address:

_____

_____

_____

4. Develop a behavior plan. Determine on-task behavior, the first teacher response, and the second teacher response (see Handout 11.6 for an example of a student behavior plan and Handout 11.7 for a blank form for the behavior plan) to delineate this information.

Colleen A. Capper, Elise Frattura, Maureen W. Keyes, Meeting the Needs of Students of ALL Abilities: How Leaders Go Beyond Inclusion. Copyright © 2000, Corwin Press, Inc.

HANDOUT 11.6. Sample Behavior Plan

Behavior Protocol: Sawyer

Ground rules for success:

- Allow time for Sawyer to process information (minimum 15 sec).
- Present information both orally and visually.
- Provide intermittent positive reinforcement.

Student behavior	Initial adult response	Follow-up adult response (+/−)
Engaged in Work • Quiet • Mindful • May stand up, but on task	• Verbal reinforcement • Primary reinforcements • Don't overdo it; does not want to be recognized	• Continued reinforcement • Or reinforcement plan
Stage 1: Initial Signs of Inappropriate Behavior • Out of seat/walks around with no direction • Constantly verbal • Looks confused	• Redirect to the task both orally and visually (e.g., "Look on the board, Sawyer. That is what you're suppose to do.") • Touch lightly on the arm • Increase process time for 15 seconds	• Modify the task so that Sawyer can meet with success • Modify the environment; check for sensory difficulties • Allow Sawyer to take a break, encourage him to verbalize need
Stage 2: Escalation of Inappropriate Behavior • Becomes argumentative when redirected • Initiates arguments with other students • Not logical • Dark circles under eyes become apparent	• Ask Sawyer what he needs: "You look like you need ____." • Use the problem/solution chart. • Use social story • Offer options for exit to a less stimulating environment • Do not touch Sawyer • Remove all stimuli (including teacher voice and eye contact)	• Redirect to another physical setting for a large motor activity; give him two win/win choices (e.g., small gym or outside) • Follow Sawyer (but do not chase) if he leaves the classroom • Uses walkie-talkies to notify office that Sawyer's in level 3/2 (third level of behavior/second teacher intervention) • Line up predetermined backup supports
Stage 3: Inappropriate Behavior Peaks • Hits things, kicks, throws • Runs/bolts • Engages in verbal challenges	• With two trained staff, remove all stimuli • Provide an environment for Sawyer to walk it off (e.g., gym, outdoors, hallways, track) • Provide tangible options for sensory integration support (do not verbalize options)	• If behaviors persist (over 1 hr and 30 min), arrange for Sawyer to exit the school grounds • Page parent; if not available, page county support person
Signs of Resolution • Sawyer allows staff to walk with him • Becomes logical	• Discuss what could have happened differently • Return to sensory diet	• Sawyer returns to his typical schedule • Staff debriefs after school to provide recommendations or changes in plan.

Colleen A. Capper, Elise Frattura, Maureen W. Keyes, *Meeting the Needs of Students of ALL Abilities: How Leaders Go Beyond Inclusion.* Copyright © 2000, Corwin Press, Inc.

HANDOUT 11.7. Behavior Plan

Behavior Plan:
Ground Rules for Success:

Student behavior	Initial adult response	Follow-up adult response (+/-)
What the student "looks like" when engaged in acceptable behaviors (e.g. on-task)		
Stage 1: Initial Signs of Inappropriate Behaviors • Able to be redirected back to task		
Stage 2: Escalation of Inappropriate Behaviors • Unable to redirect to task but able to avert Stage 3		
Stage 3: Inappropriate Behavior Peaks • Behavior is no longer within student's control		
What the student "looks like" when moving from unacceptable to acceptable behaviors		

142

Colleen A. Capper, Elise Frattura, Maureen W. Keyes, *Meeting the Needs of Students of ALL Abilities: How Leaders Go Beyond Inclusion.* Copyright © 2000, Corwin Press, Inc.

Self-Evaluation:
Leading Beyond Inclusion

Directions: Complete the following Likert-type scale by rating the level of success, as well as delineating strengths/limitations, the next steps that should be taken, and what the timeline might look like.

5 = How we do business;   4 = Increased comfort level;   3 = Beginning implementation;
2 = Emerging through conversation;   1 = Yet to acknowledge as a need

Focus Area Chapter 11: Standards for Student Behavior	Likert-type Scale	Strengths/ Limitations	Next Steps	Timeline
Major area of emphasis:				
1. All students have access to interesting and challenging curriculum (limited tracking).	5 4 3 2 1			
2. We provide students ample opportunities for independence, belonging, generosity, and mastery.	5 4 3 2 1			
3. Students with behavioral challenges are not negatively labeled.	5 4 3 2 1			
4. We have high expectations for behavior in a context of care.	5 4 3 2 1			
5. We have a schoolwide discipline policy with individually designed consequences.	5 4 3 2 1			
6. We address challenging behaviors early through early intervention.	5 4 3 2 1			
7. We involve students with behavioral challenges in all aspects of intervention.	5 4 3 2 1			
8. We work with and for families, rather than blame them or their children for their troubles.	5 4 3 2 1			

(Continued)

Self-Evaluation (Continued)

5 = How we do business;   4 = Increased comfort level;   3 = Beginning implementation;
2 = Emerging through conversation;   1 = Yet to acknowledge as a need

Focus Area Chapter 11: Standards for Student Behavior	Likert-type Scale	Strengths/ Limitations	Next Steps	Timeline
9. When a student challenges, we determine the communicative intent of the behavior.	5 4 3 2 1			
10. All educators share similar expectations and strategies for student behavior.	5 4 3 2 1			
11. We agree that teaching and learning appropriate behaviors are a long-term process.	5 4 3 2 1			
12. All educators know and use proactive behavioral strategies with students who need extra support.	5 4 3 2 1			
13. When a student challenges, support strategies include an intensive inquiry into efforts the school may have made to prevent such behaviors, going back to the student's earliest grades in school.	5 4 3 2 1			
14. We use intensive inquiry as an opportunity to consider proactive schoolwide or policy changes that could prevent such behaviors in the future.	5 4 3 2 1			
15. Functional behavioral assessments and behavior plans are written for those students needing consistency across environments and individuals to modify behaviors that are challenging.	5 4 3 2 1			

Comments:

Part III

Make the Law and Funding Work for You

Often, educators point to interpretations and applications of the law or limitations in resources as constraints to meet the needs of students of all abilities. We disagree. In Chapter 12, we show not only how traditional interpretations of the law can perpetuate segregated programs but also how rethinking legal mandates can support the diverse needs of all learners. Legal mandates are often supported by financial resources, and too often we have let budgets, rather than student needs, dictate our actions. In Chapter 13, we show how to move beyond these perceived funding constraints.

Chapter 12

Legal Supports

How Educators Can Use the Law to Meet Students' Needs

The hope that a common education might exist above politics and sectarian strife was—and is—no more than a vision. Laden with political idealism, sometimes this vision illuminated and sometimes it obscured the problems of a pluralistic, unequal society. Public education was and always will be inherently political. The high rhetoric of the Constitution advocated a basis of universal learning for sustaining the political community of a new nation. Yet, leaders were often willing, perhaps unwittingly as much as purposefully, to use new constructs of the public interest and the common good to favor some people's interest more than those of others. (American Political Science Association, 1986, p. 158)

Legal statutes, state and federal courts, and the U.S. Supreme Court have attempted to clarify and mandate equality within the public schools since the ratification of the U.S. Constitution more than 220 years ago. People of the United States proceed unassumingly to rely on the Constitution and the Bill of Rights to delineate the rights of "all people" as clarified in the Fourteenth Amendment (the right to life, liberty, and property). Regardless, the words "all children" have been, in reality only, "the majority," leaving 20% to sometimes 40% of students without equal educational opportunity and dependent on the courts to chisel away at redefining the word *all*. We continue to institute educational legislative requirements at the state and federal levels as a reaction to the denial of equal educational access for students who do not receive appropriate public education.

For example, the American Schools Act, the Elementary and Secondary Education Act, and the Individuals with Disabilities Education

Act (IDEA '97, 20U.S.C. §1401, *et. seq.*), and other global nondiscrimination legislation have been enacted to protect children whom educators have defined as other than "all." IDEA has been one of the most detailed and intrusive educational regulations enacted. IDEA provides for due process and requires a parent's signature for several permissions in the process. The courts required these protections because they understood that labeling children for special education had the potential to deny them their civil liberties. That is, the decision in *Brown v. Board of Education* argued that a separate education could not be equal.

Other nondiscrimination regulations have been applied to the public school arena but not enacted specifically for public schools. For example, Section 504 of the Vocational Rehabilitation Act of 1973 prohibits public agencies that receive federal dollars from discriminating against anyone with a perceived disability that inhibits a life function.

As we explained in Chapter 1, during the past two decades, school equity legislation has significantly affected how schools provide educational services for all students. Some students with alcohol and drug addictions have received small-group counseling and support within our public schools from Drug Free Schools legislation. Students achieving below grade level in reading and math have received small-group tutoring services from Title I. Title IX has provided female students who were denied educational opportunities based on gender access to different subject areas and extracurricular teams and events. Other students who have been discriminated against for health disorders or other life-restricting needs now may attend school and receive support because of Section 504. Many children of color no longer must attend schools separate from their Caucasian peers, thanks to the decision in *Brown v. Board of Education*. Educators have moved students with mild to severe disabilities from segregated church basements to segregated classrooms in clustered school sites, to general education classrooms with support via the provisions of IDEA. Students using English as a second language now may receive additional supports within our public schools (*Lau v. Nichols,* 1974). Such examples are only representative of some legislative changes that have broadened the meaning of "all students" in public education.

Repercussions of such legally driven equity, however, are competition, inequity, and separation. If we continue to build legal equity based on a perceived norm and those who fall short of the norm receive "other support" from legislation, then we build a system that is separate and not equitable (see Handout 12.1).

Therefore, we must move away from equity-driven legislative quick fixes and build a public school system based on equity for all. We can only accomplish such equity when we apply IDEA to all students regardless of eligibility. All students should have the same due process—that is, the right to challenge the appropriateness of educational services. All families should receive notification and be involved when schools meet as a team to discuss their children. The state and national standards across the country require all students to meet grade-level standards, be provided accommodations, or be provided alternative standards. Because of these standards, all students should receive individualized instruction and bias-free assessment in the least restrictive environment.

More specifically, we advocate for merging the Elementary and Secondary Schools Act, which dictates compulsory education and outlines local responsibilities to students, with the Individuals with Disabilities Education Act (IDEA) to provide the most appropriate services for all students. To illustrate our argument, we draw on the case of student discipline in schools and the ways we treat some students differently because of their labels, thus resulting in unfair situations for all students involved.

In a high school, three students are caught fighting in the hallway. One student receives services under IDEA, and because of the legislative requirements regarding discipline, we suspend the student for 3 days and then allow this student to return to school. The other two students do not receive services under IDEA (they are not labeled with a disability), and we suspend them for 15 days; we schedule a hearing to consider expulsion. Administrators, teachers, students, parents, and policymakers have increasingly become frustrated with this differentiation in student treatment. Such differentiation of discipline continues to be the core of much inequity within our schools. Unfortunately, educators rush to a "solution" and often argue that, in this case, all three students should receive the same punishment (suspension pending expulsion).

We agree that we should hold all students to the same behavioral standard (see Chapter 11). Here, we would follow through the process we recommend in Chapter 11, including assessing the communicative intent of the behavior of the students, the events preceding the situation, and whether harassment played a role in the situation (see Chapter 7). Then, no matter what the educators considered appropriate consequences for the students, we would provide all three students the benefit of continuing to be educated to meet the district's learning standards. That is, if expulsion were determined to be the consequence for any one of the students, the student, whether identified with a special education label or not, could continue to receive educational services from the school. Perhaps the student would receive services in a different setting, but we could deny no student an education, whether or not she or he was identified with a disability label.

Could a situation ever occur in which we need to expel a student from school and not allow her or him to receive services? What if, for example, a student murdered or raped another student at school? When we accuse a student of a crime, she or he comes under the jurisdiction of the courts. All students younger than age 18 receive education in jail according to the Compulsory Education Act. Thus we agree that a student in this case should receive the legal consequences but that we should also educate her or him (in prison) and provide psychological supports. Society does not benefit from consequences without education, whether in a classroom or within the context of an entire country. Schools routinely expel students from school, however, and do not offer them an education program. In this case, students would be better off educationally if they committed a felony. Ironically, schools are one institution that can deny children's access to education.

If, in fact, not denying educational opportunity to a student labeled with a disability is important, is it not just as important not to deny educational opportunities for students without disability labels? Why should we not work to meet the individual needs of all students? We should afford all students a free appropriate public education even or especially during disciplinary proceedings.

To create and work with legislation that can meet all students' needs in schools, we must implement the following four phases to change with support from all governmental levels—from the federal government to our local school boards (see Handout 12.2).

Phase 1: Apply Principles of IDEA to Each Student

We should not use IDEA to label students. Districts should, however, use IDEA to build equitable services for all students in the areas of due process, discipline, academic services, evaluations, teaching, and assessment practices. For example, all parents should be invited to participate in educational decisions about their child.

Phase 2: Commingle Funding Across Legislative Sources to States and Individual Districts

Alcohol and other drug abuse programs (AODA), special education, general education, Title I, and other funding sources must be commingled at the district level to meet the needs of all learners through services, rather than through segregated programs.

Phase 3:
Merge University Certification Programs
That Currently Support Separate Legislation

We must continue to ask the necessary questions about such programs. These questions will raise awareness of the restrictions and
disservice such segregated certification programs provide. Universities should not expect educators to navigate the walls between professional programs. University educators need to model the professional exchange of expertise across disciplines that characterize
practices that meet the needs of students of all abilities.

Phase 4: Merge Legislative Requirements
Under an Education-for-All-Students Act

We continue to approve legislation that is developed in isolation from
other legislation and then expect this legislation to be applied within
2 feet of each other in schools. Local districts must assist their legisla-
tures in understanding the negative effects of separate legislation
within the educational arena and move to regulations in support of all
students in the least restrictive manner.

All students could benefit from consistency in legal mandates that
support individualized instruction, bias-free assessment, and equity
across discipline. We discuss in the next chapter how funding could
support this consistency.

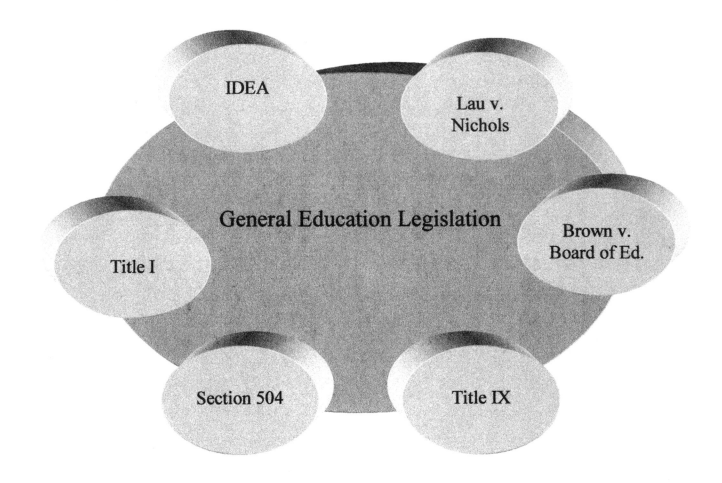

IDEA

Lau v. Nichols

General Education Legislation

Title I

Brown v. Board of Ed.

Section 504

Title IX

Handout 12.2. Four Phases for Legislative Changes to Meet Student Needs

Phase 1: Apply principles of IDEA to each student.

Phase 2: Commingle funding across legislative sources to states and individual districts.

Phase 3: Merge university certification programs that currently support separate legislation.

Phase 4: Merge legislative requirements under an education-for-all-students act.

Self-Evaluation:
Leading Beyond Inclusion

Directions: Complete the following Likert-type scale by rating the level of success, as well as delineating strengths/limitations, the next steps that should be taken, and what the timeline might look like.

5 = How we do business; 4 = Increased comfort level; 3 = Beginning implementation;
2 = Emerging through conversation; 1 = Yet to acknowledge as a need

Focus Area Chapter 12: Legal Supports: How Educators Can Use the Law to Meet Students' Needs	Likert-type Scale	Strengths/ Limitations	Next Steps	Timeline
Major area of emphasis:				
1. We are applying the principles of IDEA to all students.	5 4 3 2 1			
2. All students have the same due process rights in that they have the right to challenge the appropriateness of educational services.	5 4 3 2 1			
3. All families receive notifications and are involved when educators meet as a team to discuss their children.	5 4 3 2 1			
4. All students receive individualized instruction in integrated environments and biased-free assessments.	5 4 3 2 1			
5. If suspension or expulsion is recommended for any student, the student, whether or not she or he has a disability label, continues to receive services from the school.	5 4 3 2 1			

6. We pool legislative requirements to build equitable services for all students in the areas of Discipline Curriculum Individual evaluation practices Teaching practices Assessment practices	5 4 3 2 1 5 4 3 2 1 5 4 3 2 1 5 4 3 2 1 5 4 3 2 1	
7. We commingle funding across legislative sources at the district level. AODA Special education General education Title I Other	5 4 3 2 1 5 4 3 2 1 5 4 3 2 1 5 4 3 2 1 5 4 3 2 1	
8. Staff who have separate licenses based on separate legislation share expertise with other staff and provide support to all students.	5 4 3 2 1	

Comments:

Colleen A. Capper, Elise Frattura, Maureen W. Keyes, *Meeting the Needs of Students of ALL Abilities: How Leaders Go Beyond Inclusion.* Copyright © 2000, Corwin Press, Inc.

Chapter 13

Funding to Meet Student Needs

School districts across the country use a variety of percentage-based reimbursement formulas to pay for public education for all students. These include but are not limited to local property taxes, income taxes, state categorical aid, and the state's equalization aid. Schools receive a percentage of local property taxes and state income taxes for each student in their district. For example, property taxes may pull in 57% of a school district's revenue, and the state income tax might add another 17%. *State categorical aid* is financial assistance provided to districts on the basis of the number of students they have who can be identified or categorized under a particular label in special education. *State equalization aid* is aid from the state to communities with low tax bases in an attempt to equalize the differences between districts with low and high property taxes. These funding formulas provide the base for the per-student dollar amount used by the district.

In addition, school districts receive funding because of federal and state regulations. Such funding has been defined as entitlement dollars to alleviate any additional hardship on a district when serving the specific student population as required by the regulation. Entitlement dollars come into a district over and beyond local property taxes, categorical aid, and state income tax. For example, one way in which school districts can receive additional funding (entitlement) for special education is based on the number of students reported in the previous year's December 1 count of students who meet eligibility for special education services. For example, on December 1, 1998, Maple Grove School District serviced 420 students meeting eligibility for special education. On the basis of the state's formula, Maple Grove receives $320 per student, or a total of $134,400 in special education entitlements.

In the area of Title I and alcohol and other drug abuse (AODA) entitlement, the funding formula is established by the federal government, and money flows from it to the state. The formula is based on the number of students in the district receiving support under free and reduced-price lunches. Entitlement dollars are intended to help districts abide by federal and state regulations.

Discretionary or competitive grants are also available to districts for specific populations of students or district needs, such as serving students with disabilities in integrated environments, technology, school to work, and alcohol and drug prevention. Competitive grants typically provide educators more flexibility when structuring services and in deciding which students can be served by the grants. This flexibility is attributable to the nature of grants which is to develop innovative services for students.

In addition, funding sources have defined the ways student needs are met by designing funding formulas connected to specified teacher certifications, type of classroom environment, and number of students serviced within a specific category. This funding scheme is also known as a *teacher-weighted formula*. For example, a district may receive 40% of the cost of all certified special education teacher salaries and fringe benefits from the state.

Other states reimburse school districts on the basis of a *child-weighted formula*. That is, districts receive more money for each student who is determined to have more severe learning needs than students without a label. Receiving money based on the number of students with a disability label can result in requiring students to be labeled to receive services and sometimes in overidentifying students as a way to bolster the amount of money the district receives. At the same time, because of the strict eligibility requirements around programs, many students may not qualify for services that they, in fact, may need. As seen in the parent's letter to us described in Chapter 3, this practice results in not serving a student until the student has clearly failed in some way. For example, in most states a student may not receive services for a learning disability until that student's achievement level is 2 years behind his or her grade level. If a student has a learning disability, like the student the parent in Chapter 3 described, but is not behind in school 2 years, regardless of the history of frustration the student has experienced and despite what we know about the importance of early intervention, a student like this is typically ill-served, if at all.

Currently, educational services in most districts are set up for most students perceived to be "typical." The typical population can constitute from 60% to 90% of the student population. Supplemental or supplanting services are provided for the remaining students. For example, all elementary classrooms provide some form of reading instruction. If a student is determined to need additional assistance in reading, then in addition to his or her regular classroom reading time, this student could receive reading support before school. This before-school support is an example of supplemental services. If, instead, we removed the student from his or her reading period and provided reading instruction apart from his or her general education peers (in or out of the classroom), then that service would supplant, or replace, the classroom reading instruction.

Such mechanisms of funding have perpetuated and often initiated the separation and isolation of services solely on the basis of where the dollars originated. For example, if IDEA entitlement paid for the renovation of an elementary classroom, often we defined that classroom as a special education room, and it was off limits to students without disability labels. Computer technology offers another example of the ways we provide or restrict services, depending on funding origin. A range of funding sources currently funds computer technology in schools. As a result, educators working in special programs "claim" these computers and draw strict boundaries around the use of this technology except in the intended programs. A school building may have an AODA computer, a Title I computer, a special education computer, and an early childhood computer. Students who do not require any of these programs may not have access to them, and students who do qualify, for example, for Title I services are often barred from using a computer purchased from special education funds.

Because of the link between funding and services, many educators believe that if a student receives services from one program, then that student may not receive services from another program. For example, many districts offer a prekindergarten or 4-year-old kindergarten for students who come from a lower socioeconomic background and are determined to need additional assistance to prepare for kindergarten. Often, financial support for this program originates from Title I funds. If a 4-year-old is determined to have a disability, that child often may not participate in the prekindergarten program. Instead, we typically require that child to attend an early intervention program we have established for students with disability labels. The fear of mixing funds or of having students receive services from more than one program often results in much greater costs for the district and in curriculum and instruction that are in opposition to research on best practices.

For example, the director of student services in one rural district proudly toured us through one of his elementary schools to show how he had coordinated with Head Start and incorporated its program into this building. Head Start typically serves early childhood education students from lower socioeconomic families. The program had its own separate room, teacher, and materials. Then, with equal pride, he showed us his room designated for early childhood education students with disabilities. The room was equal in size to the kindergarten room, yet one full-time teacher and two full-time aides served only seven students in this room. The colorful room was filled with many toys, games, computers, and other teaching materials.

After we left this room, we reflected on the creative collaboration between Head Start and the school and the obvious care and concern for all students in the district. We also recalled, however, how educators and the public are frustrated by the cost of special education programs and what a waste of funds this model seemed to be. Further, this district's model violated what we know about best practice, especially for young children with and without disability labels and for children from lower socioeconomic backgrounds. That is, these children learn much more when we teach them alongside one another. Moreover, teachers learn more about serving a range of students when they work with someone with skills that may be different from their own. In this district, all the preschool students could have been served in an integrated setting, resulting in significantly greater gains in student learning at significantly reduced costs.

We know that we cannot neatly slot student needs into non-overlapping areas such as reading needs, addiction needs, or emotional needs. As we can see from these examples, local money, entitlement, categorical aid, and discretionary monies are used to supplement or supplant services for specific populations of students. As a result, educators build structures that divide and separate children and educational personnel at a great cost—financially and educationally—to the students and the public. If services for students are to be based on individual student needs and not funding mechanisms, then we must formulate funding in a manner to promote the flexibility of services without segregating students and educational personnel.

The reauthorization of IDEA mandates that services should not be provided to students on the basis of place; that is, for example, students labeled with severe mental disabilities should not automatically be placed in a separate classroom or resource room. Funding formulas must reflect the intent of IDEA and not reward segregated or separate placements (neutral placement funding formulas). This means we must orchestrate such services in a way that one to three individuals share expertise and arrange services to meet the individual needs of each student (see Chapter 9) in integrated environments. As such, creative uses of funding must promote such services, not inhibit them.

Thus far, state departments of education have not taken the lead on creative uses of funding that support seamless services to meet the individual needs of each student. Therefore, school districts must model appropriate neutral placement funding formulas for state educational departments. They can do this by merging funds at the district level to meet better a broader range of needs. In so doing, districts can synthesize services for the child rather than expect the child to synthesize fragmented services provided by adults.

To work toward neutral placement funding, we recommend the following guidelines:

- Local control of funding is essential to resolve issues creatively for all students without segregating students by needs. Just as essential as control, however, is the responsibility of local educational agencies to use the money to meet better the individual needs of all the students and not for other purposes.

- Funding sources must merge for services for all students instead of restricting services by specific funding sources and formulas.

- The funding for students with special needs was initially intended for 10% of a district's population. We now use this funding, however, for 20% to 50% of a district's population. This funding is no longer an add-on, but we must merge it with other mainstream funding sources to meet the needs of all students of all abilities.

- Equity does not and will never mean the same—because individuals are not the same. Therefore, we must not assume that we can educate every child with the same number of dollars. Equity does mean that each student receives the educational services he or she needs to be productive members of our society.

- All district leaders and staff members must be responsible for providing services for each child, rather than an administrator allocating funding after he or she has delineated the service structures for the general population.

Handout 13.1 graphically depicts the merger of funding sources, based on the above guiding principles. To meet the needs of generations of students to come, we must assess how public education facilities receive money, how we channel the funds, and how we promote or restrict services to children by funding formulas intended to assist them.

HANDOUT 13.1. Limitations of Funding Sources and Merger Recommendations

Examples of Funding Source	Current Funding	Limitations of Current Funding	Recommendations for the Merger of Dollars in Support of All Students
Title I	Follows a socioeconomic student population to allow for remedial reading/math in a proactive manner. Often funneled through the director of curriculum and instruction and student services.	• Districts often focus dollars on elementary populations only. • The word *supplants* is used within the legislation, which often forces the district to provide services through a pull-out program. These services, however, could be provided in the classroom.	Commingle funding in support of services to meet the individual needs of all students. For example: 1. Use dollars to lower class sizes and assist all teachers in the teaching of reading. 2. Use Title I dollars to hire academic and behavioral facilitators to assist current staff in meeting the needs of a diverse range of learners in integrated environments.
IDEA entitlement	Follows services for students with disabilities under state and federal special education laws. Funding is based on the number of students with disabilities. Often used to provide teacher training. Can be very beneficial for all staff if used to assist teachers in meeting the needs of diverse learners.	• Monies are often used to add staff (e.g., instructional assistants). • Monies are used to supplement needs of students with disabilities only. • Dollars are managed and allocated through the director of student services/special education.	Commingle funding in support of services to meet the individual needs of all students. For example: 1. Allocate funding to the individual schools to assist in purchasing a variety of reading materials that would be accessed by all teachers to meet the individual needs of all learners. In addition, continue to use dollars to purchase specific items for students who need unique materials to meet their individual needs (e.g., a voice-activated computer card).
IDEA early childhood entitlement	Follows services for students with disabilities ages 3 through 6 who meet eligibility for special education. The money is often used to set up classrooms and purchase equipment for students with special education needs.	• Money is primarily used in support of students who meet eligibility for special education. • Money is used to purchase materials for separate classrooms.	Commingle funding in support of services to meet the individual needs of all students in integrated environments. For example: 1. Use early childhood dollars to assist in the setup of a primary (3-year-olds through 7-year-olds) learning facility or gradeless school where the individual needs of all students occur. 2. Use early childhood dollars to assist families in providing early intervention practices within the home to prepare children better when they enter school.
Alcohol and other drug abuse programs (AODA)	Funding is based on the percentage of children receiving free and reduced lunches. The money is often used for preventive, intervention, and postintervention activities.	• Often, the money is used to pay staff to meet and discuss the needs of the district. • In addition, student favors are purchased, DARE activities are provided, postprom activities are enhanced, and so on.	Commingle funding in support of services to meet the individual needs of all students in integrated environments: For example: 1. Use AODA dollars with early childhood to implement a targeted descriptor completed by the service delivery team, such as "Children learn best when families are provided early intervention." 2. Use AODA dollars to support teachers to develop student assets.

Self-Evaluation: Leading Beyond Inclusion

Directions: Complete the following Likert-type scale by rating the level of success, as well as delineating strengths/limitations, the next steps that should be taken, and what the timeline might look like.

5 = How we do business; 4 = Increased comfort level; 3 = Beginning implementation;
2 = Emerging through conversation; 1 = Yet to acknowledge as a need

Focus Area Chapter 13: Funding to Meet Student Needs	Likert-type Scale	Strengths/ Limitations	Next Steps	Timeline
Major area of emphasis:				
1. We merge technology funds so that all students can have adequate access to computer technology to meet needs. We avoid establishing separate technology for separate programs (e.g., the "special education computers," the "Title I computer").	5 4 3 2 1			
2. We provide integrated services for preschool and kindergarten students and avoid establishing separate programs based on family income or disability labels.	5 4 3 2 1			
3. We do not place students in separate programs or segregated places (e.g., rooms, schools) because of funding; we provide services to students in integrated educational environments (neutral placement funding).	5 4 3 2 1			
4. Central office administrators merge funding sources to meet the individual needs of all students.	5 4 3 2 1			
5. Building principals merge funding sources to meet the individual needs of all students.	5 4 3 2 1			
6. Building teams merge funding sources to meet the individual needs of all students.	5 4 3 2 1			
7. Other:	5 4 3 2 1			

Comments:

Colleen A. Capper, Elise Frattura, Maureen W. Keyes, *Meeting the Needs of Students of ALL Abilities: How Leaders Go Beyond Inclusion.*
Copyright © 2000, Corwin Press, Inc.

Part IV

View the Process as a Journey, Not a Destination

In our opening chapters, we offered detailed suggestions for getting started toward meeting the needs of students of all abilities. We are all too familiar with the initiative "flavor of the week" in schools and how early enthusiasm wanes over the long haul. In Chapter 14, we suggest, however, that meeting the needs of students of all abilities can be a self-renewing practice—a practice that, instead of draining energy, continues to bring new vitality into our professional lives.

More Suggestions for School Change

We cannot continue to do what we have been doing in the name of meeting the educational and behavioral needs of each learner. We must make significant changes to save the generations of learners to come. Before educators begin to make changes in their practices, however, they need to decide first in what areas they can change and in what areas they cannot.

In this chapter, we first describe locus of control as a way of discerning priorities for change. Next, we discuss how practitioners must take a dual approach to change. Finally, we offer a conceptual framework that can help educators sort through varying stages of change on the way to creating and sustaining schools that are successful for each student.

Determining the Locus of Control

True change begins where we have the most influence, and the most influence occurs where we have the most control. Educators have prided themselves on putting students first. In putting students first, all decisions are student centered, and educators assume that adult needs are second. In practice, the reverse has actually occurred. Adults have placed their expectations on students and have expected students to perform. In some classrooms, this has proved successful: The teacher has met the child where she or he is and has assisted the child through the learning process. In other situations, however, if the child has not grasped the material, she or he has failed—not the adult, but the child.

For student failure to change, we must first change our assumptions about where change can occur—or locus of control. We conceptualize *locus of control* as a set of nested layers (see Handout 14.1). The first level of locus of control is not the student but ourselves, followed by the educational environments around us, our colleagues, then the student, encircled by the community and the families of our children (Kathy Larson, personal communication, February 5, 1998). As seen in the handout, the student is three steps away from the educator, yet we most often start with the student when we discuss change. Change must begin with the individual, and the only individuals whom educators can change are themselves.

How educators must change to teach each child may not be immediately visible, but as we walk forward, look into ourselves, and are open to new ideas about teaching and learning, we will find our way. According to Quinn (1996),

> This can occur only if we are willing to journey into unknown territory and confront the wicked problems we encounter. This journey does not follow the assumptions of rational planning. The objective may not be clear, and the path is not paved with familiar procedures. This tortuous journey requires that we leave our comfort zone and step outside our normal roles. In doing so, we learn the paradoxical lesson that we can change the world only by changing ourselves. (p. 9)

Educators spend a significant amount of time and energy on issues over which they have little control. Educators must begin with their own assumptions and their own behavior to move into service delivery changes that are beyond bandages. We must begin with where we can change. The walk may be treacherous and long for some, but until we take the first steps, we will continue to perpetuate and even promote the failure of 10, 20, 30, 40, and even 50% of our student population.

In Handout 14.2, we summarize a few key points from the book to lead beyond inclusion. For some educators, this change in roles will evolve naturally; for others, this evolution will become one of the greatest transformations of their lives. Each educator will be at a different starting point. Each educator has developed a framework or perspective from which she or he comfortably functions. For some, that perspective is in direct alignment with teaching to a range of learners. For others, that perspective is a polar opposite from where they currently function.

A Dual Approach to Change

When we move to meet the needs of students of all abilities, we must balance the need to be proactive and preventive with the need to "clean up" from past practices. As we have argued throughout this book, educators must take proactive and preventive approaches with students. At the same time, however, we must clean up practices that we once thought were effective but, given what we know now, that may not be in the best interests of students. For example, if a high school is not serving students who are behind in credits, some educators seek a solution by creating an alternative program for these students. We agree that we must meet the needs of these students. Simultaneously, however, the school must take a searching and fearless inventory of itself in deciding how to prevent this lag of credits from happening in the first place. As we explained in Chapter 6, we need to spend more time on proactive change and less time on management and reactive leadership.

One Framework for Change

We have found an adaptation of Quinn's (1996) conceptualizations of change to be helpful in our work. He portrays a cycle of transformation in four phases (initiation, uncertainty, transformation, and routinization; see Handout 14.3). Quinn states that when an individual or group desires to change, a vision develops and then people begin to take risks. If the vision becomes an illusion, then those risk takers may stop at this point. If they can move ahead into experimentation or the uncertainty phase, however, then they will gain insight and confidence about their ability to make change and can move on. This is often the level when educators panic and may decide to turn back and never move to the transformational phase of change. For example, they can become stuck with developing and continuing programs for some students instead of moving to provide services to all students. In the transformational phase, if the individual or group of individuals can move into confirmation of the vision/insight, then they can build synergy and move ahead.

Here, we begin to depart from Quinn's (1996) model. At this point, Quinn suggests that the next step is mastery of the change. We contend, however, that when we work toward meeting the needs of students of all abilities, we will never be "masters." This is because each child is unique and brings her or his own set of unique traits to the teaching-learning situation. Over time, however, although we do not have all the answers, we can become comfortable with not knowing all the answers (become comfortable with feeling uncomfortable) and become comfortable with working with students who have a varied range of abilities.

If this process falls on one person's shoulders, however, then exhaustion may occur, synergy will not take place, and transformation to new practices may not happen. With the support of each other, we can become confident about teaching to a range of students of all abilities, and this confidence can become the norm in the school.

Further, because each student brings to the teaching-learning process her or his own unique gifts, strengths, and challenges, in a school oriented toward quality teaching for each student, routinization can never occur. One primary strength of addressing the range of student needs in the change process is that teaching can never stagnate. Students who challenge our teaching routines can be our greatest catalysts for creativity and an ongoing source of rejuvenation for our continued learning.

We close with four additional suggestions we have found helpful when considering change. First, do not mandate leading beyond inclusion. The outcomes of change depend on how we do it. If we mandate something in a district or school and we tell people what the parameters are, then we imply that they do not have ownership of the initiative, that their opinion does not matter. This is why we suggest throughout this book the process of asking questions (Chapter 2) and, over time, of engaging with colleagues in conversations and then working toward structured meetings (Chapter 3). Action research (Anderson et al., 1994) can support this ongoing process of asking questions and talking with each other about why we do what we do. We can ask questions, collect data, join in conversations, facilitate structures and group processes conducive to change, and provide support and encouragement. Without losing sight of the goal of meeting the needs of students of all abilities in integrated educational environments, however, we must ultimately let go of the outcome of our efforts and our personal timeline for seeing progress toward our goal.

Second and relatedly, leading beyond inclusion should not become a crusade. It is much better to support individual schools or classrooms in the process of seeking better ways to meet the needs of all their students than to create district- or schoolwide mandates. Change is a process, a human process, and because it is a human process, it should be a respectful process.

Third, do not use the law as a threat for people to change. Although some aspects of the reauthorization of IDEA support leading beyond inclusion (see Chapter 1) and can back up this work, demanding that people comply because of the law is not the way to lasting, deep change.

Fourth, and as structural as it sounds, be sure that meetings are productive. We should run all meetings efficiently, with clear starting and ending times and with clear goals and objectives that we seek to meet each meeting. We do not want to set up meetings with wishy-washy topics and casually "see how far we get and go from there." This is not to say that we should stifle conversation and discussion by trying to stick to an agenda, but a culture of ongoing informal questions and conversations among educators can support productive meetings.

Finally, schools must do a much better job of modeling family-centered policies, practices, and change. Schools, more than any other institution in society, have as their primary focus children and their families. We are alarmed at the number of evening meetings that educators, particularly administrators, are required to attend each week—time taken away from their own families. Most schools do not provide day care for preschool children of employees. Many school leaders discourage or do not support school employees from attending school events of their children who are enrolled in other schools or districts. We often frown on educators who leave the school at their contract time and praise educators who work many long hours at the school. We should hold high expectations for educators while encouraging them to take care of themselves and their families. Because change begins with ourselves, we must take care of ourselves.

In sum, change is difficult for everyone. If change does not occur proactively, however, it will occur reactively. We can choose to plan for change and orchestrate proactive supports or allow change to happen to us and negatively affect children. We know that change is difficult for everyone, for some more than others. If change does not occur and routinization continues, however, then educators will continue to respond to student needs in a reactionary fashion that has proved itself many times not to be successful. We have one choice as professionals: to plan for change and orchestrate proactive supports. To do this, we must begin where we have the most control, and that is with ourselves. We cannot make these changes alone, however. We must enlist the support of other educators and tap into our personal systems of care to walk with us on this path. Meeting the needs of students of all abilities and leading beyond inclusion is an ever-changing journey, not a destination.

Handout 14.1. Understanding Our Locus of Control for Making Change in Education

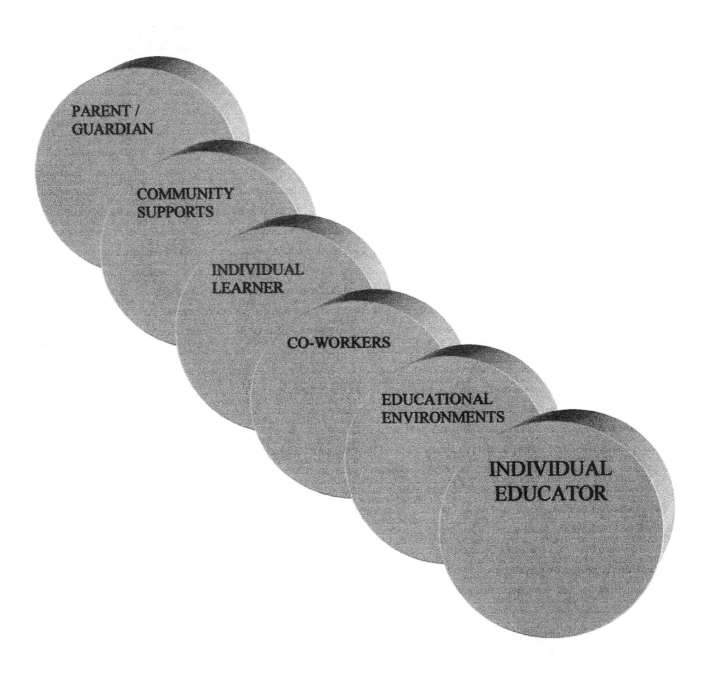

PARENT /
GUARDIAN

COMMUNITY
SUPPORTS

INDIVIDUAL
LEARNER

CO-WORKERS

EDUCATIONAL
ENVIRONMENTS

INDIVIDUAL
EDUCATOR

HANDOUT 14.2. Leading Beyond Inclusion

Traditional perspective of including students	Inclusive perspective	Beyond inclusive perspective
The problem is within students.	We use terms like *students with disabilities* and *students without disabilities*.	All students are considered gifted and challenged in varying ways.
Programs must fix students, and after students are fixed, they can return to the school or classroom.	We still rely on an "expert" model of building teams to make decisions, although at times parents and students are included more.	Curriculum and instruction are restructured to the benefit of all students.
Programs should be made more efficient and coordinated.	We search for positive problem alternatives based on student strengths.	All students are prepared to make a difference in their communities.
Educators do not take responsibility for all students in the neighborhood/building.	We advocate for students of all abilities in the classroom.	Students do not need a label to receive an education that matches their gifts and learning styles.
Students are referred and labeled to receive help.	Students with labels seldom assist students without labels.	Students do not need to fail before learning needs are addressed.
We rely on "expert" building teams to make decisions.	Labels remain intact: a definite distinction between "general" and "special" education.	All educators take ownership of all students.
The focus is on student deficits.	For students to receive services, they need a label.	Emphasis is on early instruction and intervention.
We slot students into programs.	We emphasize cooperation, collaboration, and accommodation, but the overall curriculum remains unchanged.	We limit our use of language that separates students (e.g., general, special, with disability, without disability).
Students belong as long as they do not disrupt the flow of education.	Lots of time and resources are spent on who is and who is not included and to what extent.	All students receive small-group or individual help at some point in the day to maximize their learning potential
Students have to "jump hoops" to be accepted in the school or classroom (e.g., achieve, behave, appear and act like other students).	We generally ignore issues of race, ethnicity, at-risk, gender, sexual orientation, and other student differences and their intersection.	
Lots of time and resources are spent on who does and who does not attend special programs.	The focus is on how students "fit in."	
When teachers are frustrated or unsuccessful, they blame students but do not look at the overall education for all students.		
The extent to which students are included is based on student deficits, not on how to change education in general.		
Students do not attend the school they would attend if they did not have a label.		
Administrative structures perpetuate segregation (e.g., a "special" technology committee, rather than one technology committee for all students that also addresses special technology).		

Colleen A. Capper, Elise Frattura, Maureen W. Keyes, *Meeting the Needs of Students of ALL Abilities: How Leaders Go Beyond Inclusion.* Copyright © 2000, Corwin Press, Inc.

Handout 14.3. Quinn's Transformational Change Cycle

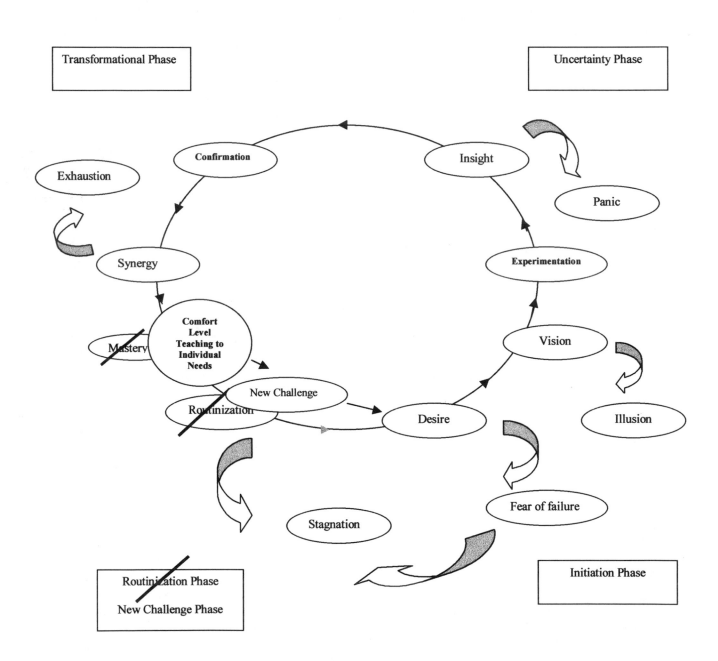

SOURCE: Adapted from Quinn, R. E. (1996). *Deep Change.*

Self-Evaluation:
Leading Beyond Inclusion

Directions: Complete the following Likert-type scale by rating the level of success, as well as delineating strengths/limitations, the next steps that should be taken, and what the timeline might look like.

5 = How we do business; 4 = Increased comfort level; 3 = Beginning implementation;
2 = Emerging through conversation; 1 = Yet to acknowledge as a need

Focus Area Chapter 14: More Suggestions for School Change	Likert-type Scale	Strengths/ Limitations	Next Steps	Timeline
Major area of emphasis:				
1. We understand locus of control and see ourselves as the first step toward change.	5 4 3 2 1			
2. We take a dual approach to change: We balance the need to be proactive with the need to "clean up" past practices.	5 4 3 2 1			
3. We are moving through the initiation phase.	5 4 3 2 1			
4. We are moving through the uncertainty phase.	5 4 3 2 1			
5. We are moving through the transformational phase.	5 4 3 2 1			
6. We are moving through the new challenge phase.	5 4 3 2 1			
7. We recognize that we will never be "masters" at meeting the needs of students of all abilities, but will appreciate how all students increase our teaching skills and creativity; we are comfortable with not having all the answers.	5 4 3 2 1			

(Continued)

173

Self-Evaluation (Continued)

5 = How we do business;   4 = Increased comfort level;   3 = Beginning implementation;
2 = Emerging through conversation;   1 = Yet to acknowledge as a need

Focus Area Chapter 14: More Suggestions for School Change	Likert-type Scale	Strengths/ Limitations	Next Steps	Timeline
8. We recognize that, by addressing the range of students needs, teaching can never stagnate and that students who challenge our teaching can be our greatest catalyst for creativity and an ongoing source of rejuvenation for our own learning.	5 4 3 2 1			
9. We do not mandate change but instead establish a process and provide support for change to happen.	5 4 3 2 1			
10. We support individual schools and classrooms to seek better ways to meet the needs of all their students, rather than to create district- or schoolwide mandates.	5 4 3 2 1			
11. We do not use the law as a threat for people to change.	5 4 3 2 1			
12. We ensure that meetings are productive.	5 4 3 2 1			
13. We seek support from each other as we work toward meeting the needs of students of all abilities.	5 4 3 2 1			

Comments:

External and Internal Assets
Developed by the Search Institute

Support	1. Family support—Family life provides high levels of love and support.
	2. Positive family communication—Young person and her or his parent(s) communicate positively, and young person is willing to seek advice and counsel from parent(s).
	3. Other adult relationships—Young person receives support from three or more nonparent adults.
	4. Caring neighborhood—Young person experiences caring neighbors.
	5. Caring school climate—School provides a caring, encouraging environment.
	6. Parent involvement in schooling—Parent(s) are actively involved in helping young person succeed in school.
Empowerment	7. Community values youth—Young person perceives that adults in the community value youth.
	8. Youth as resources—Young people are given useful roles in the community.
	9. Service to others—Young person serves in the community one hour or more per week.
	10. Safety—Young person feels safe at home, school and in the neighborhood.
Boundaries and Expectations	11. Family boundaries—Family has clear rules and consequences and monitors the young person's whereabouts.
	12. School boundaries—School provides clear rules and consequences.
	13. Neighborhood boundaries—Neighbors take responsibility for monitoring young people's behavior.
	14. Adult role models—Parent(s) and other adults model positive, responsible behavior.
	15. Positive peer influence—Young person's best friends model responsible behavior.
	16. High expectations—Both parent(s) and teachers encourage the young person to do well.

(Continued)

Constructive Use of Time	17. Creative activities—Young person spends three or more hours per week in lessons or practice in music, theater, or other arts. 18. Youth programs—Young person spends three or more hours per week in sports, clubs, or organizations at school and/or in the community. 19. Religious community—Young person spends one or more hours per week in activities in a religious institution. 20. Time at home—Young person is out with friends "with nothing special to do" two or fewer nights per week.
Commitment to Learning	21. Achievement motivation—Young person is motivated to do well in school. 22. School engagement—Young person is actively engaged in learning. 23. Homework—Young person reports doing at least one hour of homework every school day. 24. Bonding to school—Young person cares about her or his school. 25. Reading for pleasure—Young person reads for pleasure three or more hours per week.
Positive Values	26. Caring—Young person places high value on helping other people. 27. Equality and social justice—Young person places high value on promoting equality and reducing hunger and poverty. 28. Integrity—Young person acts on convictions and stands up for his or her beliefs. 29. Honesty—Young person "tells the truth even when it is not easy." 30. Responsibility—Young person accepts and takes personal responsibility. 31. Restraint—Young person believes it is important not to be sexually active or to use alcohol or other drugs.
Social Competencies	32. Planning and decision making—Young person knows how to plan ahead and make choices. 33. Interpersonal competence—Young person has empathy, sensitivity, and friendship skills. 34. Cultural competence—Young person has knowledge of and comfort with people of different cultural/racial/ethnic backgrounds. 35. Resistance skills—Young person can resist negative peer pressure and dangerous situations. 36. Peaceful conflict resolution—Young person seeks to resolve conflict nonviolently.
Positive Identity	37. Personal power—Young person feels he or she has control over "things that happen to me." 38. Self-esteem—Young person reports having a high self-esteem. 39. Sense of purpose—Young person reports that "my life has a purpose." 40. Positive view of personal future—Young person is optimistic about her or his personal future.

SOURCE: Reprinted from *What Kids Need to Succeed: Proven, Practical Ways to Raise Good Kids,* by Peter L. Benson, Ph.D., Judy Galbraith, M.A. and Pamela Espeland © 1998. Used with permission from Free Spirit Publishing, Minneapolis, MN; 1-800-735-7323; *www.freespirit.com;* ALL RIGHTS RESERVED.

Demographic Data Questionnaire

When asked to report number and percentage, it is crucial that you report both. It is impossible to make comparisons among students, schools, or other situations if you do not also report the percentage.

General Data	
1. Number of students in your district.	
2. Number of staff in your school (certified and noncertified):	
3. Number of students in your school:	
4. Number and percentage of student services staff (certified and noncertified).	
Social Class (Report number and percentage)	
5. Students receiving free and reduced-price lunches in your educational setting:	
6. Students receiving free/reduced-price lunches in other schools in your district at the same level (elementary, middle, secondary):	
7. Students identified for special education (all categorical areas) in your educational setting:	
8. Of the number of students identified for special education, how many and what percentage receive free/reduced-price lunches? *NOTE: We have found that most districts do not gather or report this information. It may be possible, however, to find such data or to calculate this information by hand.	
9. How does the response in Item 8 compare with the response in Item 5? The answers should be similar. If, for example, 60% of students identified for special education also qualify for free and reduced-price lunches (#8), and if your educational setting has 20% of its students receiving free/reduced-price lunches (#5), then students for free/reduced-price lunches are overrepresented in special education. Further, this means that, in this setting, if a student is from a lower socioeconomic family, she or he is three times more likely to be labeled for special education than other students. What social class myths support these data?	

10. Students identified as "gifted" (e.g., TAG) in your setting who receive free/reduced-price lunches: Compare the response to Item 5.	
11. Students identified as "at risk" in your setting who receive free/reduced-price lunches: Compare your response with that in Item 5.	
12. Collect social class comparison data on at least two other areas in your school/setting (e.g., PTD, Student Council, Safety Patrol, Band).	
13. What do these social class data mean? In your analysis, include the strengths and areas for improvement in serving students of lower socioeconomic classes within your school's curriculum, instruction, and culture, and ideas you have for remedying the weaknesses.	
Race and Ethnicity (Report number and percentage)	
14. Students of color in your school:	
15. Students of color in the total district:	
16. How does the information that you collected in Item 14 compare with that of the other schools within your district?	
17. Students labeled for special education (should be the same response as in Item 7):	
18. Of the number of students labeled for special education, what number and percentage are students of color?	
19. How does this number and percentage compare with those in Item 14? Analyze this in a similar way as in Item 9.	
20. Of the number and percentage of students labeled "at risk," what number and percentage are students of color? Compare the response with that for Item 14.	
21. Of the number and percentage of students labeled "gifted," what number and percentage are students of color? Compare the response with that for Item 14.	
22. Total staff of color in your school: Compare the response with that for Item 14.	
23. Certified staff of color in your school:	
24. Uncertified staff of color in your school:	
25. People of color serving on the school board:	
26. Collect race/ethnicity comparison data on at least two other areas in your school/setting.	
26a. Discuss the problems with the phrase "I don't even see the person's color."	
26b. Discuss the problems with the phrase "But we do not have, or have very few, students of color in our school/district, so race isn't an issue here."	

27. What do these race/ethnicity data mean? In your analysis, include the strengths and areas for improvement in serving students of color within your school's curriculum, instruction, and culture, and ideas you have for remedying the weaknesses.	
Gender *(Report number and percentage)*	

28. Females on the teaching staff at the
    - elementary level:
    - middle school level:
    - high school level:	

29. Females teaching science and math classes at the middle/high school:	
30. Females teaching English (and related courses) at the middle/high school:	
31. Females teaching history (and related courses) at the middle/high school:	
32. Females teaching the highest level of math students at your school:	
33. Females teaching advanced placement courses at the high school:	
34. Out-of-school suspensions or expulsions by gender:	
35. Females/males with an emotional disability:	
36. Females/males on the administrative team:	
37. Females/males at the elementary, middle, and high school administrative level:	
38. Females/males on the school board:	
39. Collect gender comparison data on at least two other areas in your school/setting.	
40. What do these gender data mean? In your analysis, include the strengths and areas for improvement in serving female and male students and staff within your school's curriculum, instruction, and culture, and ideas you have for remedying the weaknesses.	
Sexual Orientation	
41. Does your district have any active policies that (deal with) support sexual orientation?	
42. How and to what extent does your district's curriculum provide instruction related to sexual orientation?	
43. If a group of students approached your building principal and requested to begin a gay/lesbian support group, how would your principal and/or district respond?	
44. Assess your school's library/media holdings related to sexual orientation. To what extent do students in your school have access to information about sexual orientation, and what is the nature of this information?	

45. Collect sexual orientation information in at least two other areas in your school/setting.	
46. What do these sexual orientation data mean? In your analysis, include the strengths and areas for improvement in serving sexual minority students and staff within your school's curriculum, instruction, and culture, and ideas you have for remedying the weaknesses.	
Students With Disabilities	
47. Students labeled with disabilities in each grade level in your school:	
48. Do all students in your school community attend the school they would attend if not labeled special education eligible? Explain.	
49. Do some students with disabilities who do not live in your attendance area attend your school or district? Explain.	
50. Collect disability information in at least two other areas in your school/setting.	
51. What do these disability data mean? In your analysis, include the strengths and areas for improvement in serving students labeled with disabilities within your school's curriculum, instruction, and culture, and ideas you have for remedying the weaknesses.	

Reference Material for Service Delivery Teams

Funding

Investigation: The truth about special education. (1996, July). *Milwaukee Magazine, 27*(7), 38-47.

Education: The struggle to pay for special education. (1996, November). *Time,* pp. 82-83.

Service Delivery

Brendtro, L., Brokenleg, M., & Van Bockern, S. (1990). *Reclaiming youth at risk: Our hope for the future.* Bloomington, IN: National Educational Service.

Quinn, R. E. (1996). *Deep change: Discovering the leader within.* San Francisco: Jossey-Bass.

Villa, R., & Thousand, J. (1995). *Creating an inclusive school.* Alexandria, VA: Association for Supervision and Curriculum Development.

Curriculum

Reigeluth, C. (1997). Educational standards: To standardize or customize learning? *Phi Delta Kappan, 79*(3), 202-206.

Tomlinson, C. (1999). *The differentiated classroom: Responding to the needs of all learners.* Alexandria, VA: Association for Supervision and Curriculum Development.

MALCOLM SHABAZZ CITY HIGH SCHOOL
Mission Statement and
and Non-Harassment Policy
4/16/94

The mission of Malcolm Shabazz City High School is to create a **harassment-free** learning environment where all people, regardless of previous academic performance, family background, socioeconomic status, beliefs, abilities, appearance, race, gender or sexual orientation are respected. It is a school where all students are able to feel safe and are encouraged to take academic and social risks. Expectations for achievement are high and learning is viewed as life long. Curriculum and personalized instruction are multicultural. A strong sense of community exists in which students are asked to participate in school decision making and Service Learning. Fundamental to the school's philosophy are viewing the student as a whole person and strengthening the connection between the student, family and community.

NON-HARASSMENT POLICY

Malcolm Shabazz City High School was founded on the belief that the atmosphere in which you learn is as important as what you learn. To promote a productive learning environment we must encourage an atmosphere which is respectful of individual differences, so that people can learn in a functional and nonthreatening atmosphere. We insist that disagreements be dealt with in a civil manner. Therefore, the following three actions are grounds upon which harassment may be filled.

A. Physical harassment or the threat of harm against individuals or their property

B. Verbal abuse, whether it attacks an individual personality or on the grounds of race, sex, sexual orientation, background, political or religious beliefs

C. Graffiti of the above nature

Harassment is defined by the feelings of the listener/receiver of a message, not the intent of the sender. It is important that the listener respectfully notify the sender when they feel harassed.

I. Process for Dealing With Harassment

A. If a person feels harassed they can choose one of three options.

  1. Receiver should respectfully confront the sender to:

    a. Provide notice to sender how you're feeling

    b. Find out intent of sender

    c. Work out conflicts and try to reach an agreement

  2. Receiver contact advisor or other teach/staff member

    a. Staff member contacts sender and hears their version of it

    b. Staff, with receiver and sender, attempts to mediate and work out conflict

    c. Peer mediator may be used

  3. Receiver contact administrator

    a. Administrator contacts the sender

    b. Administrator, with receiver and sender, attempts to mediate and work out conflict

    c. Peer mediator may be used

B. If harassment is significant or persistent by sender to receiver

  1. Receiver fills out letter of harassment and meets with administrator stating specifics of harassment

  2. Administrator meets with sender, asking for written or verbal response (parent/guardian may BE informed)

  3. Administrator, advisor(s), and a peer mediator (as a group) will review information with sender and receiver

C. The following are possible sanctions, consequences, or responses, pertaining to individual or specific incidents, that may be decided by the group (administrator/staff/peer mediator). The sender's past record concerning harassment at Shabazz may be used in the group's decisions concerning sanctions.

  1. Mediation resulting in compromise solution for resolution of conflict

  2. Community service for sender

  3. (a) Verbal warning, (b) written warning, (c) dropped from Shabazz

4. Written warning: second incident leads to being dropped from Shabazz

5. Suspension

6. Dropped from Shabazz

7. Apology(ies)

8. Apology(ies) and sanctions

9. Some combination of the above and/or other sanctions that may fit the harassment

Sender (and parents of sender, if it is determined to be of a serious nature) meet with administrator to receive group's decision. Failing to abide by the decision leads to being dropped from our program. The decision may be appealed. (See Sec. VI)

II. Retaliation

If the student accused of harassment physically retaliates, the group will take this into consideration and if found guilty, the student will be dropped from the program.

III. Third-Person Harassment

If a person witnesses something that he or she believes is harassing to another person, he or she may initiate harassment proceedings. The third person should notify the sender. Staff must then contact the alleged victim to verify the incident. The person believed to have been harassed does not need to file harassment to agree with the complaint. If the person believed to have been harassed does not agree that it was harassment, the complaint is dropped. This does not include complaints filed by people witnessing a situation that is personally harassing. Someone who did not witness the incident cannot file the harassment.

IV. Time Limits

The student must file harassment within two weeks of the last incident of harassment. The student may use other previous incidents as well as to substantiate the claim provided these incidents are specific. We feel that a time limit of two weeks is ample time to report an incident if it is truly harassment. This will hopefully deter someone from filing a complaint as past incident.

V. Appeal Process

Sender or receiver writes a statement on why they want to appeal. They have three weeks to appeal after a decision has been made. A new group, consisting of three staff members and a peer mediator must be present for appeal (administrator will not be present). After appeal meeting the teacher can meet with the administrator and recommend dropping the harassment charge, lessen the punishment, or recommend no change from the original decision.

2/98

SHABAZZ EXPERIENCE I
Policies & Procedures

Do You Know What They Mean?

To be successful at Shabazz, there are four basic policies you need to understand and follow: nonharassment, AOD, attendance, and probation. However, "understanding" is NOT a matter of being able to complete a worksheet or take a test on what the policies are. There are real consequences for not knowing this information—ignorance can mean not getting credit in classes or even being dropped from Shabazz.

We're interested in knowing whether you have internalized the information about these four policies. Obviously, there will be "authentic assessment" at the end of the quarter when you have been successful at Shabazz. But we'd like to have you try out your knowledge on some scenarios that won't have immediate, real-life consequences for you. These scenarios were created by students from last quarter's Shabazz Experience I class. We hope you'll be able to think through these very typical "case studies" to demonstrate your understanding of the fundamental Shabazz policies.

THE ASSIGNMENT

1. If you were absent (physically or mentally) when we read through the non-harassment and Alcohol and Other Drugs policies, please be sure you get a copy of them and read them carefully.

2. On your own or with a partner (your choice), do a close reading of the Attendance Policy and the Probation Policy. Complete the worksheet that accompanies them. On this particular assignment, there ARE right answers, and they DO matter.

3. When you have completed the worksheet and read all of the policies, get a set of three or four scenarios from one of the teachers. You may work on your own, or with one or two other students. If you are in a group, you only need one set of scenarios unless you WANT to do more.

THE TASK:

A. Read each scenario, of course.

B. Write a *response* to this general question: What would happen next, according to the Shabazz policies?

C. Write your *rationale* for your answer by giving evidence from the policies.

D. Be prepared to share at least one of your scenarios and responses orally in class.

We'd like you to finish this during class on Thursday, but we may give you time to share on Friday.

You have heard a panel of "old" students explain the Shabazz non-harassment policy to you. Over the weekend, please read the policy carefully, in order to respond to the scenarios below. As you are reading, feel free to highlight, underline or write notes on the policy—it is for your use and reference.

Choose five of the following scenarios to respond to. Using your knowledge of the non-harassment policy, explain what would happen in each situation at Shabazz (ideally, of course. Sometimes humans don't behave as we would wish or expect them to!). Write your answers in complete thoughts/sentences and make sure your response would be clear to a reader.

CASE STUDY #1:
FRANK AND WALLY

Frank and Wally were both kind of young and immature; they found it hard to sit still and they tended to let off steam by running and mock fighting. One day Frank was in a bad mood and when Wally thought he'd mess with him as they usually did, Frank hauled off and punched him. What happens next?

CASE STUDY #2:   STEVE AND MELANIE

Melanie and Steve used to go together, but Melanie wanted to stop seeing Steve. However, he continued to try to get physically close to her, in the halls and in classes, touching her and kissing her though she said she wanted him to stop. What can Melanie do about this?

CASE STUDY #3:   SYBIL, CHERYL, AND ANNABEL

Sybil tells Annabel that Cheryl has been putting the moves on Annabel's man; she says she saw them at a party when Annabel wasn't around. Cheryl and Annabel have been friends for a long time, but Annabel is very convinced by Sybil. Annabel verbally threatens Cheryl, promising to beat her up after school. Other students overhear the threats. What should happen here?

CASE STUDY #4:   MAX AND MOE

Max has been threatening Moe with bodily harm every day of the school year. He never acts on it, but promises to "get Moe" when he least expects it. Moe now expects it every day. What can Moe do about this situation?

CASE STUDY #5:   ARLENE AND PHYLLIS

Arlene has filed harassment against Phyllis, who has been calling her a slut and a whore and telling other people stories about Arlene's sex life. Phyllis has been verbally warned, but she still gets in digs at Arlene every now and then. Can Arlene do anything about this?

CASE STUDY #6:
DIANE, RHONDA, AND VANESSA

Diane overhears Rhonda making remarks about Vanessa in the Center and in a couple of classes during the day. They're made in Vanessa's hearing, but to other people. Vanessa doesn't say anything, but Diane is very upset about hearing the remarks; she's offended by the language and she knows some things Rhonda is saying are not true. Can she do anything in this situation? Should she?

CASE STUDY #7:   MYRON

Myron's backpack has a number of symbols scrawled on it—including a swastika. He carries the backpack with him everywhere. Is this a violation of the non-harassment policy? What might happen next?

CASE STUDY #8:   HELEN AND JORDAN

Helen is a practicing Catholic whose faith is very important to her; she is very involved in her church and church activities. In a class discussion, Jordan makes derogatory comments about "all Christians." Helen is bothered by the comments, but no one else seems to be; in fact, most of the class shows some agreement with Jordan. How would the non-harassment policy address this?

CAST STUDY #9:   STAN AND WILLIAM

Stan and William have been enemies for a long time; they fight frequently, verbally and physically, in their neighborhood. Now they're both at Shabazz. The first day there, Stan says something to William and William threatens to get him after school. Nothing physical happens on school grounds. Does the non-harassment policy have a place here?

CASE STUDY #10:   SYLVIA AND SANDRA

Although Sylvia and Sandra have been good friends for a while, something makes them angry with one another and they can't put the friendship back together. Sylvia can't get over her anger and feels that Sandra was totally to blame. She also tells other people her part of the story and phrases it in such a way that Sandra seems to have harassed her. The story builds and, after a month, someone suggests that Sylvia charge Sandra with harassment. Can she? Should she?

Finally: Make up your own scenario that could be used with a future Shabazz Experience I class, based on the non-harassment policy. If you use real stories, please disguise the identities of the people involved.

Why the Respect Workshop?

How do we address the issue of respect? We've all been told, and we all agree, I hope, that we should respect each other. Believing in respect does not seem to be the problem. Even though we may all agree that we *should* "respect" each other, we still have problems of disrespect. The question is raised, do we really know what respecting the "other" really means?

 Given the problems of "disrespect" in the Shabazz community, it was decided that there should be a meeting of the minds to determine what "respect" is and to try to address the problem of disrespect at

Shabazz. A group was formed, made up of staff and students, and it was named the Respect Workshop Committee. After serious deliberation, the group decided that one important aspect of respect involves understanding our shared similarities In other words, we are all similar in many ways. Respecting an "other" person involves understanding and taking into account these similarities.

As a result, the Respect Committee came up with the following four skits titled:

1. We all have feelings.

2. We all need to feel safe.

3. We all have likes and dislikes.

4. We all have been shaped by our past.

The Respect Committee believes that the titles of these skits are four ways in which we are similar. The skits that will be performed here today will be examples taken from real life situations at Shabazz; situations where these similarities were recognized or ignored.

The purpose of this workshop is not only to become aware of our similarities, which we may already recognize. We are also learning to recognize situations where we are disregarding the needs of others. This is not an easy task—Shabazz is a community of individuals with different tastes, preferences, ideas, and opinions. How can we express our ideas and beliefs at the same time that we recognize our four similarities? **(We all have feelings. We all need to feel safe. We all have likes and dislikes. We all have been shaped by our past.)** The first step is to recognize that these statements are not saying that we are identical. Instead, they are stating that we have similar needs based upon our unique characteristics:

- Everyone has feelings, although they may be different from ours, they deserve recognition.

- We all need to feel safe, although circumstances of feeling safe differ for each person.

- We all have likes and dislikes, which are unique and often very specific.

- We all have been shaped by very different life circumstances that have shaped our own particular beliefs, mannerisms, ideas and opinions.

The second step towards recognizing similarities is to understand the reason Shabazz exists—its purpose. Shabazz is a community of learners. It is believed that in this community we will be able to learn from each other, to celebrate each other's differences. As a group of learners, our ideas and opinions will change, the way that we view the world will change, the way that we treat each other will change. Just as we were shaped by our past experiences, we are shaped by this community. The hope of the Respect Committee is that this workshop will help us to make Shabazz a safer place to learn, to grow and to change. By being a safe environment, it is hoped that change will be more likely. We hope that this change is in a direction toward a greater understanding of our similarities, leading, therefore, to greater "respect."

Recognizing similarities will not end the conflicts at Shabazz. Conflicts are a normal part of any healthy, growing community. However, recognizing similarities *will*, we hope, help us to solve our conflicts. Solving conflicts in our community, the Respect Committee believes, should be done in a way that protects feelings, ensures safety and recognizes differences. Knowing how to do this is not easy. Hopefully, today's workshop will help everyone to both recognize situations of disrespect and to provide examples on how to deal with these situations.

The four skits will be performed by your fellow students. Your job is to determine what you think is a good way to deal with these situations. In other words, how would you deal with this situation? Underlying this process is the question, how can we deal with this situation to better recognize the similarities that we share? Each 3rd hour class will be assigned one of the four skits to discuss and to answer the above question. In answering this question, each class will come up with a solution to the conflict represented in the skit.

—The Planning Committee

SOURCE: Malcolm Shabazz City High School (1994); reprinted with permission. Thanks to the staff and students at Malcolm Shabazz City High School.

References

Allen, J. (1995). *The relationship between organizational implementation of inclusive practices and teacher personal concerns.* Unpublished doctoral dissertation, University of Wisconsin—Madison.

American Political Science Association. (1986). *This Constitution: Our enduring legacy.* Washington, DC: Congressional Quarterly.

Anderson, G. L., Herr, K., & Nihlen, A. S. (1994). *Studying your own school: An educator's guide to qualitative practitioner research.* Thousand Oaks, CA: Corwin.

Benoy, I. (1996). How open and effective elementary school principals use vision and political strategies to influence teachers (Doctoral dissertation, University of Georgia, 1996). *Dissertation Abstracts International, 57/03,* 9361.

Benson, P. L., Galbraith, J., & Espeland, P. (1998). Forty developmental assets. In *What kids need to succeed: Proven, practical ways to raise good kids.* Minneapolis, MN: Free Spirit.

Blase, J., Blase, J., Anderson, G., & Dungan, S. (1995). *Democratic principals in action.* Thousand Oaks, CA: Corwin.

Brendtro, L., Brokenleg, M., & Van Bockern, S. (1990). *Reclaiming youth at risk: Our hope for the future.* Bloomington, IN: National Education Service.

Brown v. Board of Education, 347 U.S. 483(1954).

Brown, L., Branston, M. B., Hamre-Niutpski, S., Pumpian, I., Centro, N., & Gruenwald, L. (1979). A strategy for developing chronological age appropriate content for severely handicapped adolescents and young adults. *Journal of Special Education, 13,* 81-90.

Campbell, R., Cunningham, L., Nystrand, R., & Usdan, M. (1985). *The organization and control of American schools.* Columbus, OH: Merrill.

Capper, C. A., Theoharis, G. T., & Keyes, M. W. (1998, October-November). *The principal's role in inclusive schools for students with disabilities, empowering and democratic schools, and restructuring schools: A comparative analysis.* Paper presented at the University Council for Educational Administration Annual Conference, St. Louis, MO.

Chambers, J. G., Parrish, T. B., Lieberman, J. C., & Wolman, J. M. (1998). What are we spending on special education in the U.S.? *Center for Special Education Finance, CSEF-Brief, 8.*

Darling-Hammond, L., & Falk, B. (1997, November). Using standards and assessments to support student learning. *Phi Delta Kappan, 79*(3), 190-199.

Ellis, S. (1996). Principals as staff developers: "State development is the key to school reform": An interview with Efrain Vila. *Journal of Staff Development, 17*(1), 52-54.

Enfield, M. L. (1988). The quest for literacy. *Annals of Dyslexia, 38,* 8-21.

Erickson, H. L. (1998). *Concept-based curriculum and instruction: Teaching beyond the facts.* Thousand Oaks, CA: Corwin.

Ford, A., Fitzgerald, M., Glodoski, J., Waterbury, K., Dyer, C., Laveck, J., Messenheimer-Young, T., & Toshner, J. (1996). *Team planning to accommodate learners with disabilities.* Unpublished manuscript, University of Wisconsin—Milwaukee, Wisconsin School Inclusion Project.

Fullan, M. (1985). Change process and strategies at the local level. *Elementary School Journal, 85*(3), 391-421.

Gordon, L. (1983). What do we say when we hear "Faggot"? *Interracial Books for Children Bulletin, 14,* 3-4.

Governor's Commission on Gay and Lesbian Youth—Massachusetts. (1993). *Making schools safe for gay and lesbian youth: Breaking the silence in schools and in families.* Boston: Author. (ERIC Document Reproduction Service No. ED 367 923)

Greenleaf, R. K. (1991). *Servant leadership: A journey into the nature of legitimate power and greatness.* New York: Paulist.

Hilliard, A. (1998, Summer). The standards movement: Quality control or decoy. *Rethinking Schools, 12*(4), 4-5.

Hines, R., & Johnston, J. H. (1996). Inclusive classrooms: The principal's role in promoting achievement. *Schools in the Middle, 5*(3), 6-11.

Individuals with Disabilities Education Act Amendments of 1997, Pub. L. No. 105–17, 105th Cong., 1st sess.

Janney, R. E., Snell, M. E., Beers, M. K., & Raynes, M. (1995). Integrating students with moderate and severe disabilities into general education classes. *Exceptional Children, 61*(5), 425-439.

Johnson, D. W., Johnson, R. T., Hodne, P., & Stevahn, L. (1997). The three Cs of safe schools. *Educational Leadership, 55*(2), 8-13.

Keyes, M. W. (1996). *Intersections of vision and practice in an inclusive elementary school: An ethnography of a principal.* Unpublished doctoral dissertation, University of Wisconsin—Madison.

Lau v. Nichols, 414U.S. 563, 94 S. Ct. 786 (1974).

Loden, M. (1996). *Implementing diversity.* Chicago: Irwin Professional.

Louis, K. S., & Miles, M. B. (1990). *Improving the urban high school: What works and why.* New York: Teachers College Press.

Lunenburg, F. C., & Ornstein, A. C. (1991). *Educational administration: Concepts and practices.* Belmont, CA: Wadsworth.

Lutz, L. (1994). Coming home: One principal's perspective on inclusion. In *Society for Developmental Education in creating inclusive education for all children.* Peterborough, NH: Society for Developmental Education.

Malcolm Shabazz City High School. (1999). *Mission statement, non-harassment policy, and policies & procedures.* Madison, WI: Author.

McKee, M. (1997). A description of leadership activities of elementary school principals implementing inclusive models of special education in California public schools (Doctoral dissertation, University of LaVerne, 1997). *Dissertation Abstracts International, 57/07,* 2777.

McPartland, J., Jordan, W., Legters, N., & Balfanz, R. (1997). Finding safety in small numbers. *Educational Leadership, 55*(2), 14-17.

Mizell, H. (1995). *The new principal: Risk, reform, and the quest for hard-core learning.* Adapted from remarks at the Middle School Principal's Institute, Louisville, KY.

Morgan, C., & Demchak, M. A. (1996). Addressing administrative needs for successful inclusion of students with disabilities. In *Rural goals 2000: Building programs that work.* (ERIC Document Reproduction Service No. ED 394 767)

Murphy, J. (1994). Transformational change and the evolving role of the principal: Early empirical evidence. In J. Murphy & K. Seashore Louis (Eds.), *Reshaping the principalship* (pp. 20-53). Thousand Oaks, CA: Corwin.

National Research Council (NRC). (1998). *Preventing reading difficulties in young children* (C. E. Snow, M. S. Burns, & P. Griffin, Eds.). Washington, DC: National Academy Press.

Neville, P. K. (1999). *The social construction of disability in teacher education.* Unpublished doctoral dissertation, University of Wisconsin—Madison.

Newmann, F. M., & Whelage, G. G. (1995). *Successful school restructuring: A report to the public and educators by the Center on Organization and Restructuring of Schools.* Madison: Wisconsin Center for Education Research.

Odden, A. R., & Picus, L. O. (2000). *School finance: A policy perspective* (2nd ed.). New York: McGraw-Hill.

O'Hair, M. J., & Reitzug, U. (1997). Restructuring schools for democracy: Principals' perspectives. *Journal of School Leadership, 7*(4), 266-286.

Peterson, B., & Neill, M. (1999, Spring). Alternatives to standardized tests. *Rethinking Schools, 13*(3), 1, 4-5, 28.

Quinn, R. E. (1996). *Deep change: Discovering the leader within.* San Francisco: Jossey-Bass.

Rankin, D. (1995). The high school principal and inclusive practices (Doctoral dissertation, Temple University, 1995). *Dissertation Abstracts International, 56/06,* 2069.

Reese, S. (1997). The law and gay-bashing in schools. *Education Digest,* pp. 46-49.

Reigeluth, C. (1997, November). Educational standards: To standardize or customize learning? *Phi Delta Kappan, 79*(3), 202-206.

Reitzug, U. (1994). A case study of empowering principals' behavior. *American Education Research Journal, 31*(2), 283-307.

Remen, R. N. (1996). *Kitchen table wisdom: Stories that heal.* New York: Berkely.

Robelen, E. W. (1999, April 21). Conferees agree on revised "Ed-Flex" bill. *Education Week,* pp. 21-22.

Roberts, C. (1997). Presentation given at Sherill's Ford, NC.

Sadker, M., & Sadker, D. (1995). *Failing at fairness: How America's schools cheat girls.* New York: Touchstone.

School District of Waukesha. (1993). *Organizational responsibilities.* Waukesha, WI: Author.

Section 504 of the Rehabilitation Act of 1973, 29 U.S.C. §794 *et seq.*

Smith-Maddox, R., & Wheelock, A. (1995). Untracking and students' futures: Closing the gap between aspirations and expectations. *Phi Delta Kappan, 77*(3), 222-228.

Snow, C. E., Burns, M. S., & Griffin, P. (Eds.). (1998). *Preventing reading difficulties in young children.* Washington, DC: National Academy Press.

Sugar Creek Elementary School. (1997). *Future service delivery model.* Verona, WI: Author.

Taylor-Greene, S., Brown, D., Nelson, L., Longton, J., Gassman, T., Cohen, J., Swartz, J., Horner, R., Sugai, G., & Hall, S. (1997). Schoolwide behavioral support: Starting the year off right. *Journal of Behavioral Education, 7*(1), 99-112.

Thompson Publishing Group. (1994). *Educator's guide to controlling sexual harassment.* Washington, DC: Author.

Thousand, J. S., Villa, R. A., & Nevin, A. I. (Eds.). (1994). *Creativity and collaborative learning: A practical guide to empowering students and teachers.* Baltimore, MD: Brookes.

Thurlow, M. L., Elliot, J. L., & Ysseldyke, J. E. (1998). *Testing students with disabilities: Practical strategies for complying with district and state requirements.* Thousand Oaks, CA: Corwin.

Tomlinson, C. A. (1999). *The differentiated classroom: Responding to the needs of all learners.* Alexandria, VA: Association for Supervision and Curriculum Development.

Topper, K., Williams, W., Leo, K., Hamilton, R., & Fox, T. (1994). *A positive approach to understanding and addressing challenging behaviors.* Unpublished manuscript, University of Vermont—Burlington, University Affiliated Program of Vermont.

Villa, R. (1998). *Creative responses to students experiencing behavioral and emotional challenges: From risk to resilience.* Paper presented at the St. Louis Inclusion Conference, St. Louis, MO.

Villa, R., & Thousand, J. S. (1995). Managing complex change toward inclusive schooling. In R. Villa & J. Thousand (Eds.), *Creating an inclusive school* (pp. 51-79). Alexandria, VA: Association for Supervision and Curriculum Development.

Villa, R. A., Udis, J., & Thousand, J. S. (1994). Responses for children experiencing behavioral and emotional challenges. In J. Thousand, R. Villa, & A. Nevin (Eds.), *Creativity and collaborative learning: A practical guide to empowering students and teachers* (pp. 369-390). Baltimore, MD: Brookes.

Index

Accountability practices, district/state:
   including students in, 115
Achievement for all, goal of, 44-45
Action research, 168
   principals' use of, 48-49, 51
Add-ons, 30, 127
ADD students, 126
ADHD student programs, 14
ADHD students, 126
Administrator, general education:
   shifting personnel role, 39
Alcohol and other drug abuse (AODA) programs, 5,
      9, 13, 14, 50, 110, 150, 161
   funding formula, 156, 161
Allen, J., 48, 50
All students, 1
   one system for, 7
Alternative schools, xvi, 6, 8, 45, 100
   growth, 10
American Political Science Association, 147
American Schools Act, 147
Anderson, G., 49
Anderson, G. L., 48, 168
Anger management, teaching, 125
AODA. *See* Alcohol and other drug abuse (AODA)
      programs
Assessment:
   all-student, 88
   authentic, 89
   benefits, 121
   functional, 92, 116-118, 120, 121, 122

individualized, 92, 118-119, 120, 121
limitations, 121
performance-based, 92, 116, 120, 121
proactive in context of belonging, 119
standardized, 92, 99, 114-115, 120, 121
See also Performance exams; Portfolio assess-
      ment; Student success, standards-based
      assessment and
Assessment practices, multifaceted, 120. *See also*
      Assessment
At-risk specialists, 38
   shifting personnel role, 40
At-risk student programs, 5, 45, 58
   high school, 13
   middle school, 14
   See also specific at-risk programs
At-risk students, 103
Authentic change, 6

Balfanz, R., 77
Beers, M. K., 46, 47
Behavior:
   as attempt to communicate, 129, 137-138
   schoolwide strategies for, 136
Behavioral assessment, 132-133
   process for functional, 140
Behavioral support, intensive, 139
Behavior plan, sample, 141-142
Belonging for all, goal of, 44-45
Benchmarks, 91, 92
   versus standards, 89